Additional praises for *Ordinary Greatness: It's Where You Least Expect It . . . Everywhere*

What are you doing—or not doing—to find "ordinary greatness"? Bilbrey and Jones sharpen our focus and change our perspective with pointers that harness what can be celebrated daily. You'll find it in places you never imagined and, when you do, higher performance and increased productivity are not far away. Buy two copies of this book—one for you and one for your boss.

—Barbara Pagano, Ed.S., Founding Partner, yourSABBATICAL, Author of *The Transparency Edge: How Credibility Can Make or Break You In Business*

In the most reflective moments of our life we wonder about paths not taken and whether there still might be time to explore new territory. Ordinary Greatness is one of those rare books that allow you to think through what might yet be, both personally and in the wider spheres of existence in our families, and even in our organizations. "What If . . . ?" "Why not . . . ?" "Could I . . . ?" and once those questions begin, the tremendous voyages of our lives can begin. Greatness is there for the taking so be careful–you may not want to risk moving out of your comfort zone.

—V. Clayton Sherman, Ed.D., Chairman, Gold Standard Management Institute, Author of *Creating the New American Hospital*

What the authors offer us is a well thought out and tested strategy for moving organizations towards their full potential. The thesis is clearly presented that as we acknowledge the greatness that can be found every day right in front of us then we can create even more of what we most need in this challenging moment. What we most need is the confidence and the certainty that we can succeed and this book shows us how available that is to us if we can just take a moment to stop our rushing towards an immediate solution and fully appreciate the potential that has always been in us.

—Ken Murrell, D.B.A., Professor, University of West Florida, Co-Author of *Empowering Employees* and *Empowering Organizations*

Ordinary Greatness is an inspirational and practical book that guided each person to discover his/ her unique gifts and the courage to live their "greatness," demonstrating the highest forms of personal accountability.

—Mark Samuel, Co-Author of *The Power of Personal Accountability*, Author of *Creating the Accountable Organization*

A great guidebook loaded with lots of practical advice and strategies to help leaders actualize their potential. In a very real way, this book also shows leaders how to help others be and do more than they thought possible. And unlike many books, the techniques are easy to use—all it takes is opening your eyes to the greatness that exists right before you.

—Robert Kriegel, Ph.D., Consultant and Author, *Sacred Cows Make the Best Burgers* and *If It Ain't Broke . . . BREAK IT!*

Thank you, Pam & Brian, for reminding us about the good/bad news in discovering talent. The good news is that greatness exists all around us—"acres of diamonds" right in our own back yard. The bad news is that we can easily miss it, as it often comes disguised in ordinary packages.

—Jim Hunter, internationally best-selling author of *The Servant*

Ordinary Greatness

*It's Where You
Least Expect It . . .
Everywhere*

Pamela Bilbrey
Brian Jones

WILEY

John Wiley & Sons, Inc.

Published by John Wiley & Sons, Inc., Hoboken, New Jersey.
Published simultaneously in Canada.

For general information on our other products and services, or technical support, please contact our Customer Care Department within the United States at 800-762-2974, outside the United States at 317-572-3993, or via fax at 317-572-4002.

Wiley also publishes its books in a variety of electronic formats. Some content that appears in print may not be available in electronic books.

For more information about Wiley products, visit our Web site at www.wiley.com.

Library of Congress Cataloging-in-Publication Data:
Bilbrey, Pamela, 1954-
    Ordinary greatness : it's where you least expect it—everywhere/Pamela Bilbrey, Brian Jones.
        p.   cm.
    Includes bibliographical references and index.
    ISBN 978-0-470-46172-3 (cloth)
    1. Success in business.   2. Corporate culture.   3. Leadership.   I. Jones, Brian, 1970-
II. Title.
    HF5386.B443 2009
    658.4'09—dc22
                                                                    2009010851

Printed in the United States of America

10 9 8 7 6 5 4 3 2 1

To my family: Your love, support, and encouragement are never ending.
PB

To Melanie and my boys: Your greatness is anything but ordinary.
BJ

Contents

Foreword

*A*ntiques *Roadshow* is a television program that was particularly popular a number of years ago, and which I believe is still running. It involves people bringing their various antiques to a traveling group of experts who tell them how much their item is worth. One of the reasons why so many people watched the show was to witness that moment when one of the experts told an unsuspecting antique owner that the lamp or end table or ceramic dog that had been taking up space in their garage for the past twenty years was actually worth a small fortune.

Beyond the novelty of realizing a windfall without having to do any real work, there is much more at work here. There is just something amazing about looking at an item that you once viewed with ambivalence and seeing it anew as an object of great worth. When that item is a person, the excitement is particularly powerful.

To understand this phenomenon, consider another popular television show—*American Idol*. There are hundreds and hundreds, probably thousands, of established singers in the world, all of whom are worthy of our time and money if we'd like to hear talented voices. But we just wouldn't get millions of busy people to stop what they were doing twice a week to listen to them simply by putting them on television. But create an environment where we get to discover hidden talent among people who we wouldn't normally notice if they bumped into us on the street, and we're suddenly fascinated.

Well, within the organizations where we work, there are lamps, end tables, ceramic dogs, and pop stars just waiting to be dusted off and celebrated every day, and there is something powerful and exciting about being the one to take them out of the garage and dust them off or let them sing.

In *Ordinary Greatness,* Pam Bilbrey and Brian Jones explore this concept and provide a comprehensive and practical set of tools for excavating the hidden value and talent buried deep within our companies, hospitals, churches, and schools. They base their advice on their own substantial experience working with real leaders in real organizations where they've helped bring about excellence where others may have seen mediocrity.

But Pam and Brian do something beyond helping organizations achieve more than they thought possible, though that alone is a great reason to buy and use this book. They also provide a blueprint for us to go about changing the lives of people who work for us by helping them realize their potential and become the people they are meant to be. That is certainly one of the most worthwhile endeavors that any executive or manager can undertake. It would also make for some great reality TV.

Patrick Lencioni
Author of *The Five Dysfunctions of a Team: A Leadership Fable*

Preface

One of the world's premier violinists, Joshua Bell, had performed in such illustrious settings as London's Royal Albert Hall, the Verbier Festival in Switzerland, and Carnegie Hall. He had toured with such acclaimed groups as the Orchestre National de France, the Salzburg Mozarteum Orchestra, and the Tonhalle-Orchester. But he had never, ever done a gig at the L'Enfant Plaza Metro station in Washington, D.C.

As it turned out, his performance there on Friday, January 23, 2007 went mostly unnoticed. Yes, amazingly unnoticed. Three days prior, people had paid $100 for less than very good seats to hear him play in Boston's magnificent Symphony Hall. Several weeks later, he would accept the Avery Fisher prize as the best classical musician in America.

But that chilly day at the L'Enfant Plaza Metro station, he was incognito, unadvertised, and unknown. He appeared to be just one more street person hoping to get enough money dropped in the open violin case in front of him to pay for his next meal. What was Joshua Bell doing there? He was taking part in a fascinating project set up by *The Washington Post*. Reporter Gene Weingarten would later describe it, in his Pulitzer Prize–winning article "Pearls Before Breakfast" (April 8, 2007), as "an experiment in context, perception, and priorities—as well as an unblinking assessment of public taste: In a banal setting, at an inconvenient time, would beauty transcend?"

Granted, as Bell entered the station during morning rush hour, he was totally nondescript in appearance, wearing jeans, a long-sleeved T-shirt, and a Washington Nationals baseball cap. Positioning himself against the wall near the top of an escalator, he drew his personal instrument from its case—an 18th-century violin handcrafted by Antonio Stradivari. Placing it beneath his chin, he commenced his one-man concert. As the emotionally powerful notes of Bach's "Chaconne" filled the air (Bell describes it as "one of the greatest pieces of music ever written"), uninterested commuters hurried by. In the next 45 minutes, Bell played no fewer than six classical masterpieces as 1,097 people filed past, most on their way to work.

Noticed by a few, Bell managed to amass $32 and change (including pennies) for his efforts. A grand total of seven people tarried to listen for a moment or two. But a hidden camera videotaping the experience revealed a fascinating turn of events: each and every single time a child walked by, the youngster stopped to listen—only to be dragged off by a disinterested parent.

The experiment revealed that magnificent art was transcended by its ordinary circumstances. Or, as Weingarten put it, Bell's performance was "art without a frame." Thus, it went largely unnoticed because of the context.

This story (and a look at the hidden camera video footage) reminded us of leaders we know who, because of their busy schedule, frantic life, and overall hectic existence, walk past greatness every day because it appears so ordinary. Then we realized that far from being the exception, this has become the norm: Greatness is overlooked on a daily basis due to the way it is encapsulated. Ordinary people do great things in the business environment, but these individuals and their deeds go largely unnoticed. Leaders simply fail to grasp what is right in front of them.

This is further evidenced by clients who bring us into their organizations to solve a problem. We soon realize that they've had everything needed to successfully resolve the issue all along—they just did not see it.

The chapters that follow will analyze the invisibility of ordinary greatness, how it happens and what it is, and how leaders can learn to open their eyes and recognize it regardless of its frame or context. Joshua Bell's story is a remarkable indictment of how society has become inured to greatness. It is a wakeup call for people in all walks of life, but especially for those in leadership positions who struggle every day to keep employees engaged and passionate about their work.

Acknowledgments

We are forever indebted to the scores of clients who have touched our lives and influenced our thinking. The honor of sharing in their pursuit of excellence is humbling. We have learned so much from observing the passion, commitment, and perseverance of these good people.

We are grateful for the story of Joshua Bell, as brought to us in Gene Weingarten's *Washington Post* article, "Pearls Before Breakfast." That tiny seed was all that was needed to spur our thinking on how everyday greatness impacts workplaces across the globe. It encouraged us to document the discoveries and the lessons we have learned over the years in a book format.

Thank you to those individuals who volunteered their time to share their perceptions and stories of ordinary greatness. So often, your stories touched us in ways you will never know. Thanks also go to the hundreds of individuals who added their voices through response to our Web-based surveys.

We are grateful to our publisher, John Wiley & Sons, and especially Sheck Cho, our editor, for the support and encouragement provided that made this book a reality. Early in the manuscript preparation, we worked with our "literary angel," Ellie Smith. Imagine her patience and her talent as she worked with us to unite our voices for the book. We will be forever grateful for her guidance. Later in the process, Deb Burdick came on board and challenged us with a "newcomer's" view of the manuscript, ensuring that our blinders did not distract from sharing our enthusiasm for discovering and celebrating the greatness that exists in all our lives. Her constant encouragement, her ever present zest for life, and, of course, her superb editing skills made this book a reality. Thank you, Deb. Thanks also to Melanie Jones, our researcher extraordinaire, who never left a stone unturned and found creative ways to add interest to the text.

Thanks to Pat Lencioni and our friends at The Table Group for encouraging us to move forward with the book. A special word of thanks is also given to our many colleagues who, through the years, have challenged our ideas and added new dimensions to our work. The long weeks on the road with delayed flights, the late meetings, the intense discussion sessions, and the rigorous debates were peppered with friendship and admiration. You know who you are and we thank you.

Chapter 1

What Is Ordinary Greatness?

Yes, I saw the violinist, but nothing about him struck me as much of anything.

—RESPONSE FROM A PASSERBY WHO HESITATED ONLY BRIEFLY
IN FRONT OF VIOLINIST JOSHUA BELL PERFORMING IN THE
METRO STATION, AS QUOTED IN GENE WEINGARTEN'S "PEARLS
BEFORE BREAKFAST," *WASHINGTON POST,* APRIL 7, 2007[1]

It was not the musician, the music he selected, or the instrument he played that prevented people passing through Washington, D.C.'s L'Enfant Plaza from recognizing greatness. Instead, the common surroundings, coupled with the perceived tyranny of their schedules, seemed to keep people on their original "track" without stopping to appreciate what was right in front of them. Joshua Bell's impromptu concert was not a destination or an event for which they had planned and saved. He appeared as they were transiting through a Metro station, and because of that, his performance was somehow seen as background noise and dismissed.

Inspired by the Joshua Bell story, and intrigued by the way this phenomenon of ordinary greatness overlooked could be applied to a broader perspective (and especially its impact in the workplace), we set out to determine a definition of ordinary greatness. We first looked to stories of modern heroes, people who were catapulted into prominence—because at one point in time, their greatness was not recognized either.

The Case for Authority

The fateful day when this movie-mad child got close to his Hollywood dream came in the summer of 1965, when 17-year-old Steven, visiting his cousins in Canoga Park, took the studio tour of Universal Pictures. "The tram wasn't stopping at the sound stages," Steven says. "So during a bathroom break I snuck away and wandered over there, just watching. I met a man who asked what I was doing, and I told him my story. Instead of calling the guards to throw me off the lot, he talked with me for about an hour. His name was Chuck Silvers, head of the editorial department. He said he'd like to see some of my little films, and so he gave me a pass to get on the lot the next day. I showed him about four of my 8-mm films. He was very impressed. Then he said, "I don't have the authority to write you any more passes, but good luck to you."

The next day a young man wearing a business suit and carrying a briefcase strode past the gate guard, waved and heaved a silent sigh. He had made it! "It was my father's briefcase," Spielberg says. "There was nothing in it but a sandwich and two candy bars. So every day that summer I went in my suit and hung out with directors and writers and editors and dubbers. I found an office that wasn't being used, and became a squatter. I went to a camera store, bought some plastic name titles and put my name in the building directory: Steven Spielberg, Room 23C."[2]

Spielberg's call to ordinary greatness was asserting itself; his mindset of authority so convinced the people he encountered at the studio that no one ever questioned his right to be there! As a matter of fact, he worked there for weeks before he was finally offered a job.

In the face of seemingly insurmountable odds—his youth, inexperience, and anonymity—he rose to the occasion by refusing to be defeated. Though it would be years before it was recognized, Spielberg instinctively knew that he had greatness in him. His air of authority allowed him to be accepted.

Do we question people whom we instinctively perceive to have authority, even though a title or formal designation might be lacking? No; rarely, if ever, do we challenge them. Instead, we respond to their attitude of being in charge almost automatically. It might be a characteristic, a hallmark of greatness to come, yet we seldom recognize it for what it is.

A Harbinger of the Future

Early in his life, one of the character traits of Sir Winston Churchill was his belief in himself. From age 22 to 26 he served in the military, first as a member of the cavalry and then as an officer in the infantry. While he fought in several wars during this time period, coming under heavy fire at the front line, he escaped injury. What was most interesting about his experiences in combat, though, was his outlook. After one battle, he wrote his mother: "I was under fire all day and rode through the charge. You know my luck in these things. I was about the only officer whose clothes, saddlery or horse was uninjured . . . I never felt the slightest nervousness."

His "luck in these things" he interpreted as Divine Providence. He wrote, "I shall believe I am to be preserved for future things." And later, "These are anxious days, but when one is quite sure that one is fulfilling one's place in the scheme of world affairs, one may await events with entire composure."[3]

Is it possible that those who will someday demonstrate greatness are better at interpreting their destiny? Is this ability to be sure about one's purpose in life a characteristic of ordinary individuals who respond to extraordinary circumstances with courage, who rescue people from burning buildings, and who save comrades from war's peril? Perhaps if each of us could hear the inner voice of ordinary greatness, it might be easier to recognize it in others.

A Desire to Help

Every day people perform acts of ordinary greatness that we fail to recognize. The Little League coach who unfailingly gives the worst players a chance at bat; the couple who adopt a child with grave physical problems; the healthcare worker who spearheads an annual drive to collect books for an inner city school . . . there are countless examples of ordinary and overlooked heroes among us. But these acts are propelled into our consciousness by the circumstances.

In 1982, Air Florida Flight 90 went down in Washington, D.C.'s icy Potomac River in the midst of a snowstorm. A federal employee on his way home from work watched incredulously as the plane clipped a bridge and plunged into the water. Lenny Skutnik could have stood by, waiting for rescue workers to save as many as they could, yet he swam out to rescue a drowning stranger.

The water was 29 degrees that day. As Skutnik watched a crash victim fail again and again to grasp a rescue basket from a helicopter, he went into the river and swam 30 yards to rescue her. Later he would say, "It was just too much to take. When she let go that last time . . . it was like a bolt of lightening or something hit me—'You've got to go get her.'"

There were several people that day who also performed feats of heroism: a helicopter pilot who endangered his own life while rescuing others; a medic who climbed out to help a victim too weak to save herself; two bystanders who went into the water to assist people; and one of the plane's passengers, who drowned after passing the lifeline numerous times to others.

The publicity-shy Skutnik was never at ease with the accolades for his bravery. "I wasn't a hero," he protests. "I was just someone who helped another human being. We're surrounded by heroes. What made this different was that it was caught on film and went all over the world."[4] Yes, we are surrounded by ordinary greatness, embodied in heroes who make a profound difference in others' lives. We seldom see this greatness for what it is, though, unless—as in Skutnik's case—it visits us in our homes on the nightly news.

Could you have done what these people did? They were common, everyday people who performed great acts, driven to help others despite the peril to themselves. They might never have been recognized were it not for the circumstances that flung them into heroism, situations they responded to as if they were predestined for them.

Hardwired to Rescue

University of Illinois at Urbana-Champaign law professor David Hyman conducted a four-year study about the willingness of average Americans to help others in need. Wondering whether U.S. law should require citizens to help each other in times of emergency, he made an interesting discovery: Rescues outnumber non-rescues 740 to 1 each year.[5] "This study shows you don't need laws to get people to rescue one another. They seem to do it themselves," Hyman said. "Americans are much better than the law expects them to be. . . . [The study suggests that] people are hard-wired to rescue. It's an instinctive response. People see someone else in peril and they will jump in, almost regardless of risk."[6]

Definition of Ordinary Greatness

Our definition of ordinary greatness evolved over the course of writing this book. Finally, we settled on "superior and often unrecognized characteristics, qualities, skills, or effort found in a person who may be otherwise undistinguished; sometimes discovered in a response to unexpected circumstances." Perhaps the easiest way to describe ordinary greatness is that it is most often uncelebrated, sometimes possesses an element of nobility, and is rarely on display. In fact, when we celebrate true ordinary greatness (see Exhibit 1.1), it is because it has managed to transcend its invisibility.

People who exhibit ordinary greatness elect to put forth an abundance of personal effort when they find themselves in extraordinary, demanding, or special circumstances with the opportunity to make a difference. They do so without reservation, answering a call that comes from deep within. The desire to be in the spotlight is never a factor. They demonstrate resilience in the face of adversity, persistence in the face of great odds, and a determination to live the values they hold most dear.

Or•din•ar•y Great•ness
Superior and often unrecognized characteristics, qualities,
   skills, or effort found in someone who may be otherwise
   undistinguished; sometimes discovered in response to
   unexpected circumstances.

Exhibit 1.1   Ordinary greatness defined

Former prisoner of war Bob Blair says he had an "epiphany—to get volunteers to help him grow nutritious food for the needy." According to ABC News, the organization that named Blair one of their "Persons of the Year," Blair noticed there were an awful lot of people, hundreds of thousands of people, who are "food insecure, meaning they don't know where their next meal is coming from." Between June and December 2008, Blair estimated he had harvested about 35 tons of vegetables with the help of 3,100 volunteers.[7]

Ron Clark, a teacher who "never wanted to teach; all I wanted was a life filled with adventure," also embodies such determination. After teaching fifth grade in Belhaven, North Carolina for five years, he saw a television program about a school in East Harlem, New York that was having trouble attracting good teachers. He immediately packed up his car, drove to New York, stayed at the YMCA, and searched out a school like the one he had seen on television. "When I started teaching there (New York City's P.S. 83, in Spanish Harlem), people at the school said it was the worst class they had seen in 30 years," Ron recalls. "There were so many discipline problems in the classroom I couldn't get the kids' attention. They didn't respect me, they didn't respect each other, nor [did they respect] the other teachers." Ron recognized the way adults take things for granted when dealing with kids. "We're constantly telling them to behave or be respectful, but we're not taking the time to show them what we expect," Ron states. He came up with a list of 55 rules for his classroom—how to give a firm handshake, how to go on an interview, how to use proper etiquette, and how to be humble and not arrogant, among others. By making his expectations clear and investing himself in the lives of his students, Ron not only taught unforgettable life lessons, he lived them. Have high expectations from others, but higher ones for yourself. Invest yourself in the potential you know is there, and find a way to relate to other people.[8]

The common theme we found that transcended all the interviews and behaviors people shared was this: Ordinary greatness knows no boundaries. The limitations of age, education, talent, and culture do not apply. These individuals are the generous humanitarians we never hear about; they are the great leaders who stay in the background; they are the unrecognized employees who quietly carry an organization to success; and they are the brave individuals who respond to a disaster behind the scenes. Ordinary greatness is everywhere, in the most common of circumstances, waiting to inspire and motivate us—the key is to recognize it!

In the words of American poet Walt Whitman, "Can each see signs of the best by a look in the looking glass? Is there nothing greater or more? Does all sit there with you?"[9]

We often overlook the ordinary greatness that is right before us.

- How do you define ordinary greatness?
- What are the clues that lead you to discover ordinary greatness?
- Have you passed by greatness only to discover it later?

Chapter 2

Ordinary Greatness Observed

It was all videotaped by a hidden camera. . . . The people scurry by in comical little hops and starts, cups of coffee in their hands, cellphones at their ears, ID tags slapping at their bellies, a grim danse macabre to indifference, inertia, and the dingy, gray rush of modernity.

Even at this accelerated pace, though, the fiddler's movements remain fluid and graceful; he seems so apart from his audience—unseen, unheard, otherworldly—that you find yourself thinking that he's not really there. A ghost.

Only then do you see it: He is the one who is real. They are the ghosts.

—Excerpt from *Washington Post* article
"Pearls Before Breakfast"[1]

Granted, the reasons people do not see ordinary greatness are easy enough to grasp. However, it is important to be able to characterize ordinary greatness and understand what it is all about. This is the first step in taking off the blinders: recognizing ordinary greatness and immeasurably enriching our lives as a result. Nothing is more meaningful to a leader than witnessing greatness in an employee who was personally coached. This is, after all, why we are called to lead.

Having scoured modern-day hero stories and conducted individual interviews, we had come closer to a definition of ordinary greatness. However, when it came to linking the concept of ordinary greatness to the workplace, a bit more research was needed. We started by looking at previously collected data. One of the sources that immediately caught our attention was the data collected from various orientation programs. During the course of their orientation with a new employer, we surveyed employees to determine the characteristics most important to them in defining a great leader and a great co-worker. Every other week, the class of new employees undergoing orientation is asked, "What makes a great leader?" The answers have been collected over years and, when they are trended, several traits or characteristics bubble to the top: honest, trustworthy, energetic, caring, supportive, and visionary. The great leader is someone who leads with conviction, but with a deep compassion and respect for those who follow. Great leaders are thoughtful, compassionate, empathetic, dedicated, and decisive.

A second question, "What makes a great co-worker?" provided additional insight. The descriptors included: always gives that extra effort; will be true to his or her word; and is not out for the glory. Other employees told us that the best colleagues are kind, considerate, and put others first; they have a good sense of humor and do not take themselves too seriously; they have a good work ethic. We even heard about an employee who purchased a set of tires for a disadvantaged coworker!

Our Survey

While each of the stories in Chapter 1 offers fascinating aspects of ordinary greatness discovered in individuals who later came to prominence, we wanted to uncover ordinary greatness as it exists in the unsung heroes all around us, the everyday people who are making a difference in the lives of others. So we conducted a series of interviews with more than 75 individuals from all walks of life. We first asked, "Who are three people who come to mind that you would consider as possessing greatness, and why?"

Interestingly enough, the interviews generated some common themes. The leading responses included: Gandhi, Martin Luther King, Mother Teresa, and Jesus. Other popular names included Jimmy Carter, Bill Gates, Abraham Lincoln, and Oprah Winfrey. As we pursued the "why" part of the question, we found that each of these individuals was larger than life. Each had a well-established reputation; some were frequently represented in the media; others were historical figures with a compelling story; some were religious role models. All were well-regarded for their ethics and morals or for their leadership and business success, but mostly for their desire and commitment to help their fellow man.

We learned about Karla Gergen, a Minnesota educator who wrote about her impressions of ordinary greatness in the life of Mother Teresa in an article for the Minneapolis-St. Paul *Star Tribune* (see Exhibit 2.1).

Karla Gergen: Heeding the call to ordinary greatness
Meeting Mother Teresa was a lesson in doing small things with great love.

By Karla Gergen
My first thought was that she was smaller than I thought she'd be. She was in a wheelchair at the back of the room, her recent illness having taken obvious toll and also the cause of her absence at the other masses we had attended. Our ride to church had taken longer than expected that morning, so we rushed right by her in our late arrival. It wasn't until about halfway through mass that I even noticed her.

"Oh, that's her," I thought, and then my mind went elsewhere.

After mass, I was preparing to leave when my friend Therese noticed people lining up and suggested we join them. When I asked what the line was for, she just shrugged and said, "Let's find out." So we did.

Then someone came along and asked everybody in the line to kneel down, and we did that too. Soon, one of the sisters brought her out in her wheelchair and rolled her slowly along our kneeling bodies with heads lowered for blessing. She briefly touched each of our heads as she said an individual prayer.

And that's how I came to be able to say that I met Mother Teresa.

Despite the famous name and face, it's not my strongest memory of my month in Calcutta, far from it. It was my other experiences that made the deepest impressions on me: working side by side with women who've cheerfully given up everything they own and their whole lives to take care of the poor; early morning walks past sleeping lumps on the sidewalk who are slowly coming to life; a mother holding up her baby to me, desperately begging for help, and me just walking away because I was so overwhelmed I didn't know what to do.

Exhibit 2.1 Karla Gergen's story
Source: Used with permission of Karla Gergen.

But you don't want to read these stories. Or rather, I don't want to write them. It's easier to write about my celebrity sighting. After all, that is what we made her—a celebrity—and I eventually learned that meeting her was the kind of story people liked to hear.

Even so, I don't tell it very well. She was one of the reasons I chose to go to Calcutta, but I hadn't been star-struck like I thought I'd be. Her ordinariness was engulfed in the chaotic beauty and suffering of the city.

By her lack of impression on me, I came to understand not that she is less important than we make her out to be, but that we are all more important than we let ourselves be. She'd be the first to say so. One of her most frequently quoted expressions says, "We can do no great things—only small things with great love." She knew that what we call greatness is found not in fame but in what we do each day, the simple and ordinary ways we live our lives.

Seven months after I returned home, 10 years ago this Wednesday, I heard on the news that she had died. I cried, though I still couldn't tell you why. It might have been that grief we feel any time someone good leaves us. It might have been in remembrance of Calcutta, what I had seen there and how it opened my eyes to how big and beautiful and horrible this world is. It might have been because it reminded me of what that Sunday morning had taught me, and I wondered whether I was living up to it.

She was just a little woman who did what she could for others and loved God. Fact is, I know lots of people like that, and from more than a brief touch a decade ago. It is their blessings—my mother kissing my forehead, a conversation with a friend who's on fire for justice, a homemade thank-you card from a student—that matter to me. These blessings remind me that I too am called to average, daily, ordinary greatness in hopes that someday, when I am old and weakened, others will be just as unimpressed by me.

Karla Gergen, Minneapolis, is a teacher.

Exhibit 2.1   (Continued)

We found Karla working at an orphanage in El Salvador—proof that ordinary greatness knows no geographical boundaries.

Missing from the list, however, were people like you and me, the everyday "Joe," the commoner whom all of us touch and are touched by each day. So we asked a second question: "Who are the three people you personally know who possess greatness, and why?" This is when the richer, heartfelt stories came to light, many of which brought tears to our eyes.

These were stories about mothers, fathers, siblings, and grandparents; they were about church pastors, nurses and doctors, teachers—they were about normal people who had made a profound impact on someone's life.[2]

Leaders were mentioned as well, such as the chief executive officer (CEO) who transformed a dying manufacturing facility of 630 employees from a dismal 43% performance rating to 108% in one year. This leader engaged employees at all levels, unleashing their creativity and enthusiasm to turn their plant around. He removed tribalism and created a seamless operation and culture that continues to be an example for other facilities, even in challenging economic times. When he had to tell staff that despite their hard work they would not receive their bonuses, 630 employees gave him a standing ovation. He was, and is, we were told, humble, driven, and extremely talented.

There were numerous mentions of everyday leaders who were considered great because of their belief in the potential of others and their commitment to help develop that potential.

At one of our client sites, the new CEO, Bill, still in his first 90 days in the position, told us that he was concerned about his marketing division. The division got good results and represented the firm well, but Bill told us, "Other marketing vice presidents with whom I have worked have been very vocal, dynamic people who kind of 'chew up the scenery.' But Sally, the marketing vice president here, rarely talks in meetings and is a bit of an introvert. There is no way she can be successful, can she?"

Our recommendation to Bill was to take a day and follow Sally around as she met with suppliers, ad agencies, referral sources, and key customers. Not only would this educate Bill about the business, its customers, and the market, but it would give him a chance to get to know Sally a little better and allow him to make a better assessment of her capabilities. He offered to spend the day with her, and she gladly agreed.

The day after their tours and site visits, we called Bill to ask him how the day had gone. He told us that he had clearly been wowed by Sally's ability, marketing savvy, and relationship-building skills with key suppliers, customers, and prospects. During the day, one of the leaders of an ad agency they had visited told Bill, "Don't be fooled by Sally. She appears to be quiet and unassuming, but when it comes to fighting for what is best for your company, she's a tiger!" Bill told us that he had learned a real lesson about his own blinders and preconceived notions about how a successful marketing vice president should behave and look. "I had allowed it to become about things other than results," he said.

At one of our client sites in the western United States, we were introduced to a man named Bailey. Now, Bailey was not someone easily overlooked, for he had been stricken with a childhood disease that rendered one side of his body useless and had limited his mental development to age ten. In many places, someone like Bailey would be passed over for just about any job, but at this client (a hospital), a human resources manager named Tim and a food service director named Betty teamed up to not only hire Bailey, but give him the very important job pushing carts of cooked food from the kitchen to the cafeteria. If you don't think that job is important, remember who eats at hospital cafeterias: not only employees, but often loved ones of patients who are at their most vulnerable.

Every day, Bailey would push his cart up and down one of the main corridors of the hospital, saying hello to every single person he would pass. In this way, he became a role model for the other employees of the hospital who began to tell themselves, "If Bailey can say hello to me and every other person he sees, then maybe I can, too." This movement began to take off in the hospital, and everyone began greeting each other in the hallways. A small thing, you might say, but this kind of ordinary graciousness can make a big difference to someone who is with a loved one in the hospital or even seeking treatment themselves.

Bailey's movement took off so amazingly that when someone did not say hello, they really stood out. Often after Bailey greeted people, if they passed him without responding in kind, Bailey would follow them and in his sweet, innocent way, ask, "Hey, Brian—I said hello, and you didn't say hello back to me—what's wrong?" Talk about accountability!

Bailey once repeated this treatment to the CEO of the hospital, who had walked past him and, self-absorbed, failed to return Bailey's greeting. Of course, Bailey was no respecter of titles in this regard, so he followed the CEO, and said, "I said hello, and you didn't say hello to me. What's wrong?" Of course, this forced the CEO to stop and say, "You know what, Bailey, you're right. I didn't say hello to you. I guess I got carried away in my own thoughts. I'm sorry." When the CEO told us this story, he said, "In this way, Bailey taught me a lesson about accountability and the fact that everybody is watching me all the time. I'm glad he had the courage to confront me. In so many ways, he is living proof that what we are building here is worthwhile."

Who knows how many people Bailey has touched at their weakest, saddest, or most distant moments? He definitely made an impact on our lives. We are glad Tim and Betty saw ordinary greatness in Bailey and set him free to make a difference.

Words from the Wise

Then there was Cher, a 21-year-old salesperson at a cellular phone store I (Pam) had the opportunity to meet after my BlackBerry died. While waiting for "the next available person," I overheard Cher and a colleague passing the time by sharing well-known quotes and guessing the author. I inserted myself into the conversation and asked if they knew any good quotes on greatness, thinking that perhaps my Saturday would not be totally wasted, and I would come away with a tidbit for this book.

Immediately Cher responded with a quote from Shakespeare's *Twelfth Night*: ". . . be not afraid of greatness: some are born great, some achieve greatness, and some have greatness thrust upon 'em."[3] Intrigued with the profound words from this young adult, I asked if she had a few minutes to chat about her thoughts on greatness. When asked the question about the three people possessing greatness who immediately came to mind, Cher responded: "Marilyn Monroe, my mom, and Cynthia, a friend of my mom's." I was surprised but delighted that she mentioned people from her personal life as two of the three.

To Cher, Marilyn Monroe was a larger-than-life figure representing immense talent and perseverance. But when she spoke of her mom, her voice changed, and her eyes lit up. "She is the greatest person. She is always there for me and never judges me. I know she wants what is best for me and I know that I can always count on her, no matter what. She loves me unconditionally and always will. She's my mom."

It was the story about Cynthia, however, that showed this young lady's maturity and insight. Cher told me of Cynthia's impact on her outlook on life. "She is the happiest person I know. She is dying of cancer and she is still the happiest person I know. She spends her time helping others. I have learned so much by watching the way she lives her life. I only hope that I can live my life with the same grace and love."

In the responses to the question about personally known individuals who possess greatness, the themes that emerged were consistent. Repeatedly we heard about people who served as role models, were supportive and nurturing, and possessed the courage of personal convictions. We heard about grandparents who raised a family single-handed; a friend addicted to drugs who turned his life around; and a co-worker who adopted six needy and medically challenged children. We learned about an employee who helped a colleague in need due to illness. On her own personal time, the employee raised more than $1,000 for the co-worker by coordinating a bake sale and other fund-raising events.

One interviewee told of a nurse she knew by first name only. Facing her mother's imminent death, the interviewee and her family stayed around the clock at the hospital for several weeks. During that time, they experienced the care and concern offered by the medical personnel. One nurse; however, really caught their attention. She was kind, gentle, and caring in all her interactions with both the mother and the family. One of the last days of her mother's life, this nurse clocked out at the end of her shift but came back to the unit to spend the final two hours with the mother and her family. The support the family experienced made a significant impression, so much so that the interviewee has since "found a calling" in volunteering at a hospice to help other families in their time of need.

A colleague told us about Jackie, always a quiet, unassuming member of the marketing team. She worked hard, did a great job editing the company's newsletter, but kept to herself most of the time. Consequently, many of us were surprised to learn of Jackie's work in the community. Only when she asked for a few days off did we learn of her commitment to a group home for mentally challenged kids.

She had supported the group home for many years, spending each Saturday taking the kids to events and activities and teaching them self-help skills like doing laundry and shopping for groceries. The two days off she requested were to take the kids to Disney World for a vacation. Jackie had put some of her own money toward the expenses and found others to financially support the trip. Our marketing department was so inspired by Jackie's extraordinary commitment to these kids that they pooled their dollars and had special t-shirts and duffle bags printed for each kid to take on the trip. Because of Jackie's commitment, our team realized we could do more to help others. As a result of her quiet, unselfish example, we created an adopt-a-family program, and each month we collectively provide a food basket and a bag of household necessities for a local family in need.

We heard about Susan from another colleague. "When I first met her," said our colleague, "I wasn't all that impressed—in fact, I was a bit underwhelmed by her, just as I expected, given what I had heard from others. She seemed to fumble over her words and had a habit of rambling on forever. Her physical appearance seemed to reinforce her reputation of not being well organized. She dressed in baggy attire and, while an attractive woman, she never wore makeup, nor did she seem to have what one would call a hairstyle.

"Quite honestly, I didn't have high expectations for working with Susan. I was concerned that I would have to micromanage her work to get the results we needed. But as we began to work on multiple projects, I found her contributions to be quite valuable. Her dedication to the work was obvious, and her willingness to learn was refreshing.

"The more we worked together, the more I realized that Susan had an extraordinary intuition for making difficult business decisions. She consistently and rationally evaluated options and determined the best course of action. I found my initial impression of Susan's lack of organization to be wrong. In fact, she was quite the opposite. I began to assign more projects to her team and before long she garnered a reputation as the go-to person in the company, willing to take the lead on the toughest projects. When the time came to fill a newly created administrative position, Susan was everyone's obvious choice." Our colleague was able to overcome an initial impression of Susan and discover the ordinary greatness that already existed in her, providing an opportunity for

Susan to excel and for the organization to capture the potential of this employee.

One person who responded to our survey gave us her very own personal and powerful perspective: "I define ordinary greatness not by things done in the spotlight but by what is done in the quiet, seemingly insignificant moments when the world is not looking." It seems people have discovered that one key to ordinary greatness is this: There is no limit to what can happen when we do not care who gets the credit.

The Effect of Blinders

We asked a final question of those we interviewed: "Which of the two questions was the most difficult to answer and why?" Almost without exception, the interviewees indicated the question that probed for people they personally know or have known was more difficult. Why? As one insightful person shared, "They are only great to me; I don't know if others would see them that way." Another said, "With people we know, we see their strengths, but also their weaknesses." Yet another person explained, "It is harder to perceive greatness in people you see every day. Sometimes it creeps up on you."

This is the effect of the blinders to which everyone is subject. Remember, all of us are predisposed to associate greatness with how it is packaged, something the media greatly impacts. It creates our heroes for us by portraying the rich and famous in an elevated context. Never mind that their personal lives are often less than idyllic. Their flaws are either hidden or presented to us in a way that falsely influences us. It is so much easier to identify greatness in the famously successful and seemingly superhuman individuals who dominate the airwaves and tabloids.

Bias and preconceived ideas also come into play here—the partiality that prevents our objective consideration of a person, an issue, or situation. We view those closest to us in a different light and are unduly influenced in our interpretation of their actions. Someone we perceive as demonstrating ordinary greatness might not qualify as such to a stranger.

Consider the story behind international cosmetics giant Avon. The company's founder, David McConnell, was born in 1858 in Oswego,

New York. He planned to become a math teacher, but instead began selling books door to door in New York in 1879. As an incentive to customers who allowed him into their homes and listened to his sales presentation, he gave them a small gift—a vial of perfume. With the aid of a local chemist, he actually created his own perfume brand, which was quite popular with his customers—in fact, more popular than his books. McConnell discovered that while his books were a one-time purchase, his perfume generated repeat business.

Young McConnell decided to create a company to sell the perfume. He named it Avon because his hometown in New York, Suffern on the Ramapo, reminded him of William Shakespeare's home, Stratford-on-Avon. McConnell launched his company, Avon Calling, in 1886. By 1887, he had 12 female employees selling 18 fragrances. At the end of his life in 1937, Avon had a sales force of over 30,000 representatives and sales volume was in the millions. Today, Avon is still a leader in national sales of cosmetics and perfumes.[4]

McConnell's real genius was in the people he selected to distribute his products. Others might view rural housewives with no sales experience who could only devote a portion of their time to work as liabilities. McConnell saw them as the foundation of his multinational company.

He clearly understood the concept of ordinary greatness.

Canadian hockey enthusiast and Royal Canadian Air Force medical officer Dr. Sandy Watson saw Olympic gold in a makeshift team of amateur hockey players.

In 1948, Canadian hockey officials decided to skip that year's Olympic Winter Games. This news so upset Dr. Watson that he took the initiative to create a team where none existed. "When I read the headline saying we—this great hockey nation—would not be sending a team, I was offended," he said. "And I thought maybe I could do something about it."

Professional hockey players were ineligible for the Olympics, so within a year Dr. Watson assembled a group of hockey-playing airmen. At the end of the 1948 Winter Games, the Royal Canadian Air Force Flyers had overcome tremendous odds to finish with seven wins and one tie, earning them Olympic gold and a place of honor in Canada's Olympic Hall of Fame.

Dr. Watson went on to become one of Canada's eminent ophthalmologists. Described as "a driving force," he is proof there is no limit to our ability to succeed when we invest ourselves in the potential of those around us.[5]

Remember, the sum total of our upbringing, life experiences, and learning results in preconceived ideas about people and their behaviors. These blinders are why we find it a challenge to answer the question, "Who are the three people you personally know who possess/possessed greatness, and why?"

Succeeding Despite Blinders

One of the areas in which the average person can sometimes be trusted to spot ordinary greatness is the movies. Sure, the big summer popcorn blockbusters with lots of explosions and car chases always seem to draw a crowd, but big Hollywood budgets and media hype do not always translate to box office receipts. Some recent examples of movies with lower price tags that resonated with the movie-going public and made money for their creators are *Slumdog Millionaire*, *Little Miss Sunshine*, *An Inconvenient Truth*, and *Juno*. These are "ordinary" films in many ways, but audiences saw greatness in their messages, or at least in their entertainment value.

Noticing this trend, David Carr wrote in *The New York Times*, "It is a truism of the (movie) industry that making even a bad movie is hard, so making a great one must be near impossible. But the odds curiously seem to go up when the odds are against the filmmaker. Part of the reason so many great movies come from outside the studio apparatus is that the lack of big shooting budgets and 'help' from the people signing the checks forces filmmakers to innovate. Ultimately, you can't manufacture cinematic excellence; you can only enable it."[6]

"You can't manufacture excellence; you can only enable it." It seems that filmmakers on their own, with smaller budgets, still produce hits because they do not have the luxury of blinders. They cannot afford *anything* that would stand between them and their artistic vision. Also, they are separated from the Hollywood bureaucracy, with its "dailies," "notes," and "help," so the directors and producers can pursue what appears to be ordinary greatness. Yet, to audiences, these films carry ideas and thoughts that are timeless. And in that sense, their greatness transcends the ordinary and becomes part of the time capsule for an entire generation.

As people work around you, for you, and with you, is your help encouraging greatness or standing in its way? Is your legacy a big-budget blockbuster with lots of wind and action that is unmemorable (see half of what is playing at your local megaplex right now, it seems), or is it a small-budget movie with a heart and an ordinary but timeless message?

Blinders are natural inhibitors that keep us from seeing ordinary greatness in those around us. While inherent to all leaders, the key is recognizing them and being aware of their effect.

Ordinary greatness is found in the eyes of the beholder.

- Who are the people you first think of who possess ordinary greatness?
- Why did those individuals come to mind?
- Name one person who has had an impact on your life whom you would characterize as great? What was the impact this individual made?

Chapter 3

Why People Do Not See Ordinary Greatness

There was a musician, and my son was intrigued. He wanted to pull over and listen, but I was rushed for time.

—Sheron Parker, IT Director, regarding her
three-year-old son's reaction in the Metro
station when Bell performed[1]

One of the most intriguing aspects of Joshua Bell's Metro station performance story (as discussed in the preface) is his impact on the children who encountered him that day in the Metro station. Unfailingly, they wished to stop and listen to him. Was it Bell's charisma that drew them, the intricacy of the sounds he was producing, his magnificent violin, or the total experience that bespoke his greatness to them? More to the point, how could a youngster perceive greatness when an adult did not?

Children are immersed in what lies before them—their experience level is such that they are insatiably curious and perpetually tuned in to new experiences. They are more open to learning (kids can master a foreign language or a musical instrument much faster than adults), are able to focus on the process as well as the results, and are highly adaptable.

They possess a sense of wonder and discovery that allows them to be creative in their perceptions, and they frequently ask "Why?" and "Why not?" They have not yet acquired the various forms of blinders that adults often wear, nor do they limit themselves or those around them. The candor and transparency of children has been the subject of any number of humorous books and television shows. Although parents are sometimes embarrassed by what their children say and do, children innately know the art of genuine, unfettered communication. Philosopher and inventor R. Buckminster Fuller made the insightful comment, "All children are born geniuses; 9,999 out of 10,000 are swiftly, inadvertently degeniusized by grownups."[2]

Actor Will Smith says of his son, Jaden, "He changed my performance. You know, when you really capture your greatness, there's going to be something childlike about it. There's going to be something at play, not at work, and watching him I rediscovered that thing that made me successful with The Fresh Prince (of Bel Air)."[3]

Actor Christopher Reeve (1952–2004) once said, "Some people are walking around with full use of their bodies, and they're more paralyzed than I am."[4] This chapter focuses on the blinders that paralyze your ability to see greatness in places where it is least expected (see Exhibit 3.1). As a leader, if you could remove these barriers, it would

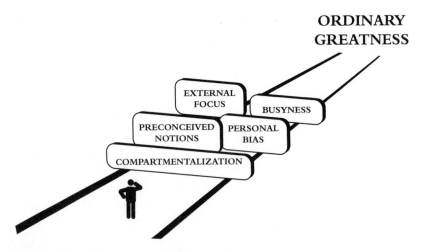

Exhibit 3.1   Blinders to recognizing ordinary greatness

be a much greater investment than any seminar on developing leadership potential. In a sense, all the greatness you need in your organization or company is already right there in the "Metro station" with you. But are you in too great a hurry to get to your train on time? Is what lies through the turnstiles of your day preventing you from pausing and recognizing the greatness that lies before you? Or do you casually breeze by and toss a few pennies in its direction, rubbing shoulders with greatness, but not grasping its value and the ways it might be leveraged for greater personal and organizational success? How you answer these questions of leadership may clue you in to how—or whether—you recognize ordinary greatness.

Compartmentalization

The first blinder that keeps us from recognizing ordinary greatness is compartmentalization, classically portrayed in the Academy Award winning movie *Good Will Hunting*. Matt Damon played the role of a janitor who worked after hours cleaning classrooms at an Ivy League college. His lowly station in life masked his brilliance.

During the course of mopping floors and emptying garbage baskets, he noticed a complex and intricate mathematical problem written on a classroom blackboard. The professor had set the problem as a challenge for his students. Time passed, the problem remained unresolved, and eventually Damon's character was unable to resist; chalk in hand, he solved it. The next day, the excited professor asked the student responsible for the resolution to step forward for well-earned kudos. As classmates looked around, no one rose. The professor posed another problem as bait, and Damon character's identity was uncovered. But the incredulous professor did not believe it. How could a mere janitor manage to solve a mathematical equation that baffled a classroom of highly educated and privileged students?[5]

The professor was simply reacting in the same way in which every one of us quite often would: he prejudged a person based on appearance, and compartmentalized based on circumstances. The very last place he expected to find greatness was in the school's janitorial department. The bottom line is: If greatness is in a place you do not expect it, you do not see it. "As soon as most of us hear or read something, we tend to immediately classify it in our minds as true or false, good or bad, right or wrong. While that is not necessarily a bad property for a manager, it is deadly for a leader," states Steven Sample in his book *The Contrarian's Guide to Leadership.*[6] Why? Because as leaders, if our minds are already divided into distinct "patterns" or compartments, there is no room for thoughtful, objective consideration of alternative approaches or solutions.

We have observed what we consider a great mystery: the application of compartmentalizing among very talented senior executives with whom we have worked. How could these leaders fail to see the greatness in their associates? Yet it happens, all the time. For example, one of our colleagues, an amazingly gifted consultant and advisor on the West Coast, lamented that he saw a lot of improvement opportunities at the church he had been a member of for years; but no one in the church leadership believed that a fellow worshiper they saw every Sunday, someone who lived among them, could possibly be capable of advising them to make improvements. They compartmentalized him as one of them and focused instead on the expertise of a consultant from another town.

We reminded our colleague that a great teacher named Jesus Christ could not draw a crowd in his hometown of Nazareth, where instead of being the King of Kings, he was "Joseph the carpenter's kid." And perhaps this bothered Jesus, because he said, "A prophet is not without honour, save in his own country, and in his own house."[7] Jesus knew and taught that compartmentalizing was an element of the human psyche, never to be removed, but always to be managed and guarded against.

Preconceived Notions

The blinder of preconceived notions—opinions formed without adequate evidence—is the result of a complex neural process. The human brain is composed of a network of billions of tiny cells called neurons that communicate with one another through electrochemical impulses. Estimates differ, but most scientists suggest the number of neurons in the human brain to be in the neighborhood of 100 billion. These neurons are circuits for the brain's information processing. However, the brain mediates the data it gets by virtue of biological, psychological, and social factors.

Social factors—your upbringing, life experiences, and learning—condition you to perceive things in a certain way and be immune to other possibilities. You believe that certain things are true; you come to expect them and judge or act accordingly. An example of a preconceived notion in the business world would be that a chief financial officer (CFO), whose job revolves around the concreteness of numbers, will not be a highly creative individual. Yet we have met many CFOs who shattered that notion and were, in fact, quite imaginative.

Another example of a preconceived notion is the recent Wall Street scandal and meltdown. Certainly Americans had the preconceived opinion that our financial system was healthy and working well. After all, the market had a long history of stability and countless examples of self-made millionaires. Record numbers of people were homeowners, Wall Street traders and mortgage brokers were making lots of money—why question things? Yet when the evidence was in, people were shocked and dismayed to learn that their views were so far off base.

In psychology, preconceived notions or thoughts based on past experience are called premature cognitive commitments (PCCs). The three elements of PCCs are:

1. *Premature.* Arriving at a conclusion without sufficient analysis or preparation
2. *Cognitive.* The process of learning, becoming acquainted with, or knowing something; occurs consciously and unconsciously
3. *Commitment.* A lasting opinion or conviction that becomes a filter for processing information and forming opinions

Put simply, premature cognitive commitments—forming conclusions based on perception or habit, without first obtaining enough facts to make sure our perspective is accurate—also contribute to a false sense of safety and security. They are the equivalent of locking our minds into a certain position, like a photograph, and making that locked position our instinctive point of reference from which other opinions are formed. PCCs commit us to thinking and acting in certain ways without stopping to analyze why, because we are conditioned to do so. Think about getting dressed in the morning. Do you carefully consider which leg to put in your pants first? Most likely not, because the act of getting dressed has become so deeply ingrained that it results in "natural" or "automatic" behaviors. Often PCCs are perspectives or actions we adopt because they made sense at one time; we hold on to them even though they might have grown outdated or irrelevant. In the workplace we often find this situation with committees that at one time had a specific purpose, but over time evolved into nothing more than a meeting to review what had been reviewed in the meeting before. The meetings continue because "we always meet."

The advantage of PCCs is the ease with which you perform daily activities; on the down side, they establish boundaries of which you're unaware, maintaining a state of ignorance that keeps you from straying beyond the limitations imposed upon your thoughts.

There is a story illustrating this concept that we have told to many groups. In India, as baby elephants undergo obedience training, they are tied with an iron chain to a huge tree. Then the size of the chain and the tree is gradually reduced. Ultimately an adult elephant can be tied with a flimsy rope to a green plant and is unable to escape. Life experience has imposed the commitment in its body-mind that it is in a prison!

Similarly, in an aquarium filled with fish, when clear dividers are inserted, the fish quickly adapt to the limits of the divided aquarium. When the dividers are removed, the fish swim only to where they know the glass dividers have been—and no further.

This is how PCCs influence your life. You treat these deeply embedded convictions—of which you are usually not even aware—as truths about your existence. Rarely do you question them, examine them, or consider how they might be influencing you. They are deeply buried mindsets that predetermine possibilities, closing off alternatives and options.

In some cases, positive cognitive commitments produce a positive result. Former President Ronald Reagan operated with the assumption that everyone he encountered would like him. This belief was, to him, a positive cognitive commitment. As a result, even his enemies were attracted to him socially. Democratic Congressman and Speaker of the House Thomas "Tip" O'Neill commented that while he opposed Reagan's policies, on a personal level, "I find it impossible to dislike the guy."[8]

Let us go back to the story of the elephant for a moment. While the creature's life experience had conditioned it to believe that it lived within a tiny, finite space, that cognitive barrier comes down in the event of a life-threatening situation. When facing immense danger such as a fire, the elephant will almost always break free of the self-imposed shackles and run. The new knowledge (heat, fire, danger) triumphs over the conditioning.

How can we find a source of new knowledge to help us overcome the barrier of preconceived notions? Let us consider what the Johari Window has to teach us. It is a highly useful model describing how human beings communicate and relationships evolve. Picture a four-paned window dividing personal awareness into a quadrant of different modes: open, hidden, blind, and unknown (see Exhibit 3.2).[9]

The first pane, openness, represents what we already know about each other. The second pane consists of information that I know about myself but keep hidden from you. The third pane is the things that you know about me of which I myself am unaware. The unknown pane represents things I do not know about myself, nor do you know about me—in other words, collective ignorance.

According to the Johari Window, being placed in a new situation can often impact the fourth quadrant. It can result in the discovery of knowledge or information previously unknown to either one of us. The novel setting or state of affairs helps to raise the window pane of

	Known to Self	Not Known to Self
Known to Others	OPEN what we know about each other	BLIND what you know about me of which I am unaware
Not Known to Others	HIDDEN what I know about me but keep hidden	UNKNOWN what neither of us knows about me

Exhibit 3.2   Johari Window

openness and shrinks the unknown pane, resulting in personal growth in our relationship with that individual.

Seeking new experiences that expose you to situations and people you would never otherwise associate with can expand your personal awareness and knowledge of human beings. In turn, you realize that what you think and act on unconsciously is not always valid. This form of self-development may be the first step to correcting preconceived notions.

Ultra-marathoner Dean Karnazes, who runs ten marathons in a row—without a break—deals with his blinders one step at a time. "I sat down at mile 240, and I literally could not get off the curb," he recounted. "I thought, how am I gonna run 22 more miles? And the answer is: baby steps. I said, 'First, stand up.' That took like three attempts. Then, 'Make it to the stop sign.' Then, 'Make it to the trash can.' Pretty soon I was clicking off the miles. I ran mile 262 in 6 minutes 30 seconds." He discovered that sometimes the secret to discovering ordinary greatness just takes the commitment to do it this minute, this hour, this day.[10]

Take a proactive approach and resolve to remove this blinder before an employee resigns and you are left wishing that person's talents had not been ignored and his or her ordinary greatness had been recognized; or before the staff member whose true capability has never been explored ceases to be engaged and simply goes through the motions of the job. Leaders walk past greatness in employees and associates every day. It is incumbent upon them to be open to the evidence of it.

Personal Bias

The word *bias*, which has its origins in the French language, originally meant *slant*. Bias has come to mean a partiality that prevents objective consideration of a person, issue, or situation. How you process information can be slanted by presumptions that influence your view. In other words, bias affects your perceptions of people and their capacity for greatness.

Bias has many aspects. The first is familiarity. It is often referred to as "common knowledge." You want to believe that with which you are most familiar; therefore, longstanding acquaintance with a person or situation gets little scrutiny. Even if that knowledge is false, it probably will not be questioned because it is familiar. The flip side of this is that something unfamiliar is disbelieved or rejected.

Consider the following: Facing a long delay in her flight home after a tiring business meeting, Marge went to the airport gift shop and bought a book, a coffee, and a small package of gingersnap cookies. The airport was very crowded, and she found a seat in the lounge area next to a stranger. After reading for a few minutes, she became absorbed in her book. She took a cookie from the package and began to drink her coffee. To her great surprise, the stranger sitting next to her calmly took one of the cookies and ate it. Stunned, she could not bring herself to say anything, nor to even look at the stranger. Nervously, she continued reading. After a few minutes, she slowly picked up and ate the third cookie. Incredibly, the stranger took the fourth gingersnap and ate it; then to the woman's amazement, he picked up the package and offered her the last cookie. This being too much to tolerate, Marge angrily picked up her belongings, gave the stranger an indignant scowl and marched off to the boarding gate, where her flight was now ready. Flustered and enraged, she reached into her bag for her boarding pass . . . and found her unopened package of cookies! How quick we are to jump to conclusions and judge others' ideas and behaviors.

Another aspect of bias is the influence of personal experience. Someone can tell you about a person, event, or situation, and even offer up proof to boost his or her position or view of the circumstances. But if you have experienced the same thing, you are inclined to accept your own conclusion over that of the other person.

There is a story told of a woman preparing to cook a roast. Before placing it in the oven, she sliced an inch off the end of the meat.

Her daughter, watching her mother, asked, "Mom, why did you cut an inch off the end of the meat before you placed it in the oven?"

"I don't know," replied the mother. "My mother always cut an inch off a roast before she put it in the oven."

Curious, the mother called the grandmother to ask why she cut the end off a roast before baking it. The grandmother had no explanation for why she cut the end off roasts before baking them. "My mother always did it," she said.

Finally, the mother and the grandmother got the great-grandmother on the phone. The grandmother asked, "Mom, why did you cut an inch off the end of the roast before baking it?"

The great-grandmother replied, "I cut the end off the roast because my pan was too small to fit the whole thing!"

A third aspect of bias is selective perception, which can alter our view of reality. Say, for example, you go out and buy a white car. All of a sudden, everywhere you go, you see white cars and quickly come to believe it must be the most popular color. Perhaps your annual review by the boss was less than favorable. Anything he or she says in the future about your work is suspect, even if it is complimentary! One consequence of this aspect of bias is that people tend to look for and believe the information that supports their opinion while rejecting information that conflicts with it. The actual facts hold little weight, because personal beliefs prevail.

The impact of the bias blinder in business dealings can be quite damaging. An excellent *Harvard Business Review* article indicates that "most companies examine the potential pitfalls at some point during the merger and acquisition (M&A) process, but often not with the same degree of insight and strategic rigor that they build into their initial case for the deal."[11] The article further outlines common biases that surface during due diligence, such as the confirmation bias, driven by people's desire to seek out information that validates the deal, and the overconfidence bias, which leads executives to submit an early bid that the company is then forced to work within to close the deal no matter the factual information that may be contrary. They suggest that successful deals are made only when executives are able to step back and take an unbiased approach to negotiating a merger or acquisition.

Bias plays a big part in the difficulty that organizations experience as they attempt to implement change. To teach the power of this blinder, we educate our clients on what we call the *group mindset*. We tell them there are three kinds of employees with respect to driving change (see Exhibit 3.3).

In any organization, introducing change reveals three different types of people. Based on a children's story from long ago, we call it the "Tator" Principle:

1. *Facilitator.* Positive people who are fully on board and ready to try something new.
2. *Agitator.* Negative people who are resistant to any change and ready to stir up trouble as a smokescreen for maintaining the status quo, believing that management's job is to protect them from change, not expose them to it.

Facilitator
Fully on board and ready to try
something new

Agitator
Resistent to change; ready to stir up trouble
as a smokescreen for keeping the status quo

Spectator
Waiting to see where the majority goes
before falling in line

Exhibit 3.3   Group mindsets

3. *Spectator.* These are generally reasonable people who will wait to see where the majority goes before falling in line. Is the change working? If so, they will hop on. If not, they will join the naysayers.

The challenge for leaders is figuring out how to deal with the second group of people. Management will find it difficult to engage them in the process because of their bias and their selective perception that leadership is not to be trusted; they make a lot of noise and, if not dealt with at some point, can bring the change effort to its knees. Not understanding the sheer power of bias, and despite our advice, leaders often attempt to win over these negative people with facts, logic, bargaining, and other tactics doomed to fail.

Leaders who do grasp the concept spend the first 90 to 180 days of any change effort with the first group of positive people. As a result, they succeed in dealing masterfully with all three constituencies. To the undecided group, it appears the positives are winning because they are getting the most attention from management. Then as the positive group grows, the negative ones can be dealt with from a position of strength, because most of the employees now support the change and the naysayers look like the ones who are out of touch. This is how cultures are changed—by leaders who pay the most attention to the positive greatness already in the company.

A final aspect of bias is being too quick to come to conclusions. Again, research tells us that generalizations are formed about people or circumstances after minimal experience. Yet these few elective examples are deemed to be representative of the whole.

For five years, from 1977–1981, actress Suzanne Somers played the role of dizzy blonde Chrissy Snow in the sitcom *Three's Company*. Her character left an indelible impression in viewers' minds. I (Pam) for a brief period traveled with Somers, and in reality, outside the role, she is a very successful business executive. She is also a well-read, articulate person; a gourmet cook; an author; and a cancer survivor. Instead of being immersed in all the trappings of a Hollywood lifestyle, Somers is someone who, like most of us, looks for the best ways to remove cat hair from furniture and foregoes a stylist in favor of doing her own hair. Yet what people remember best about Suzanne Somers is the role she played for five years in the late 1970s and early 1980s. How many of us would care to be remembered forever for our "roles" during those years?

Generalizing from limited exposure and basing further interaction on those initial impressions is something every leader must guard against. We have worked with many leaders who lost credibility with their staff because they were too quick to come to conclusions. One of the favorite aspects of our consulting work is coaching leaders who have participated in a multi-rater, 360-degree feedback survey. They receive anonymous feedback from their boss, their staff, and their peers, which they then compare to their own perceptions about self-performance. Here are some of the comments we have seen:

- Joe makes decisions based not on reality, but on the last thing he heard on the subject.
- Everyone knows that all you have to do is be the first one to get to Susan, and she will take your side.
- Once Ben forms an impression, it is impossible to move him off of that, even if the facts prove him wrong.

Bias can serve as a great source of personal limitation. Familiarity, personal experience, preconceived ideas, and generalization can negatively influence information that comes into your life. Any or all of these can unfairly influence your interpretations of people and their capacity for greatness.

External Focus

Whether or not you realize it, you tend to associate greatness with how it is packaged. It may be the high-powered executive, the wealthy, the politically powerful, the sports hero, movie star, or those who move in elite circles. The external trappings are accepted and rarely questioned or examined in depth. For example, one of the components of our work as management consultants is the personal interview we do with executives. Everyone believes these leaders are at the top of their game, garnering a six and even seven-figure salary, working in a well-appointed office (with a window of course), living in a beautiful home, and possessing the obligatory sailboat. But when we talk with these executives, we find they are confused, miserable, and disillusioned about their work. Contrast them with Darren, the cheerful, down-to-earth custodian. Darren invests himself fully in his work, emptying the trash and cleaning the floors. Even though Darren is an employee of a contracted custodial firm, he knows he is making a real contribution to the functioning of the office and is a valued member of the team. He often brings interesting articles he has read to various people and is quick to tell a good story. It is not uncommon to find a cake or plate of cookies that Darren has baked and left in the break room for sharing.

External packaging is especially true in the world of the elite professional athlete. The persona often screams "petulant superstar," yet that assumption can be very deceiving. Consider Terrell Owens formerly of the Dallas Cowboys. To the world, Owens had it all. Yet all was not as it seemed. In 2007, it was widely reported he suffered from an accidental overdose of prescription medication. Owens claims that upon his return to the team, his head coach never even asked him about the incident or how he was doing. Yes, to us he was a supreme athlete and a monumental asset to his team. But something was missing in Owens's life—a relationship with his boss and the assurance of support behind the scenes. While his coaches and teammates were invested in Owens's contribution to the team, his behavior off the field spoke volumes about the absence of accountability and true leadership in Owens's life.[12]

In contrast, Pittsburgh Steelers owner Dan Rooney takes a vital interest in his team members on and off the football field.

"It started with my father," Rooney said. "He gave me the values. He treated players, coaches, general staff as people. He was concerned about them."

That culture now permeates the entire organization—a sort of ego-free zone in which players and coaches can occasionally seem as if they're competing for a Nobel prize in humility. "We don't care who gets the credit, and all we want to do is win," Steelers Coach Mike Tomlin said.

Rooney has consistently looked not just for skilled ballplayers but for athletes who would hold themselves accountable to each other and the community. "Those are the kind of people he assembles here, and it makes it a fun place to work," Tomlin said.

The result has been stability and continuity. Now in his second season, Tomlin is the Steelers' third head coach in 40 years—testimony to the Rooneys' loyalty, patience, and understanding of what it takes to build a winning team.[13]

Busyness

Americans are workaholics, addicted to schedules, timelines, and calendars. We rush to catch airplanes and trains, book rental cars, and check our BlackBerries. Every year, Expedia.com commissions its "International Vacation Deprivation Survey," conducted by Harris Interactive and Ipsos Redi. The 2008 survey revealed that Americans are likely to give back more than 574 million vacation days, with each employed U.S. adult age 18 and older expected to leave an average of four vacation days on the table. The study also revealed that one-third of Americans do not always take all of their vacation days, despite more than one-third reporting that they feel better about their job and more productive upon returning from vacation.[14]

Even when leaders and employees do go on a holiday, they tend to take the job with them, thanks to laptops, e-mail, and cell phones. The demands of working usurp almost everything else in daily life. It seems that the United States has become a nation of people who cannot stand *not* to be busy and productive in some manner. We are continually multitasking, networking, chairing committees, and raising funds. Even positive activities such as soccer games, play dates, and tutors lead to overscheduled youngsters. There is no time for reflection, for endeavoring to see beyond the next byte of time . . . to perceive ordinary greatness.

Several British newspapers ran a story a few years ago about an employee of a New York publishing firm who had been dead at his desk for five days before anyone noticed. A proofreader at the firm, the man supposedly suffered a heart attack in the open-plan office he shared with 23 other workers. He quietly passed away on a Monday, but nobody noticed until the following Saturday morning when an office cleaner asked why he was still working during the weekend.

Yes, the story later proved to be an urban myth, widely circulated because so many people believed it to be true. It was taken as gospel because it reflected what work lives have come to be: obsessed with being and staying so busy that there is no time for reflective thought about what is happening before your very eyes.

It has been said that the average speed of vehicles traveling through New York City in 1903 was 11 miles per hour. The average speed of vehicles traveling through New York City in 2003 was 11 miles per hour.

Are we really working faster?

American journalist and author Hunter S. Thompson (1937–2005) made this observation: "I've been there, and I can tell you that the fast lane is littered with countless smoldering wrecks."[15]

The Recognition Factor

Okay, so there are many reasons leaders don't recognize ordinary greatness: compartmentalizing people; wearing cognitive blinders; being biased in favor of internal markers; seeing only the external packaging and not what lies beneath; ignoring potential in favor of the known; and being victims of the perpetual busyness that inhibits contemplation. Yet the main reason we fail to see ordinary greatness is the setting. Quite simply, it appears in a context where it is not expected.

Remember Joshua Bell (from the preface)? There he was, one of the world's foremost artists, a violinist of international acclaim, playing for all he was worth in the midst of a Metro station. Yet he wasn't recognized because he was in a place where he and his greatness of craft were least anticipated!

Greatness is all around us. The lesson of this chapter is that it may not always be where we expect to see it. It is often in the next cubicle, in the Metro station, and even in us!

The late Charles Schulz (1922–2000), creator of the *Peanuts* comic strip, was responsible for a well-known exercise to help people reflect on the source of true significance in life. He would ask people to name the last five winners of the Heisman Trophy, the Miss America Pageant, and the Academy Awards for best actor or actress. As individuals struggled for answers and failed miserably, Schulz then asked the group to name the people who have most inspired them, teachers who have most influenced them, and friends who have helped them. This time the answers were quickly forthcoming. Those who really make a difference in our lives are the ones who have had a personal impact, the ones who cared.

American philosopher William James (1842–1910) once said, "The greatest use of life is to spend it for something that will outlast it."[16]

Discovering greatness in ordinary situations requires us to release patterns of thinking that limit possibilities.

- What needs to happen for you to see greatness every day?
- What blinder is the most challenging for you?
- How do you break down the "brick wall" of daily routine to gain new perspectives?

Chapter 4

How Leaders Open
Their Eyes to Ordinary
Greatness

Three minutes went by before something happened. Sixty-three people had already passed when finally there was a breakthrough of sorts. A middle-aged man altered his gait for a split second, turning his head to notice that there seemed to be some guy playing music. Yes, the man kept walking, but it was something.

—EXCERPT FROM "PEARLS BEFORE BREAKFAST,"
WASHINGTON POST, APRIL 7, 2007[1]

A s a leader, how do you know if you are prone to a particular blinder that keeps you from recognizing and fostering ordinary greatness in employees? What's more, what can you do to remove these blinders and allow yourself to be a better leader?

In this chapter, we will eavesdrop on a series of high-powered executive meetings as a new chief executive officer (CEO) coaches his team about blinders. The dialogue is followed by a series of self-discovery assessments to help you identify whether or not you are prone to that particular blinder, and the specific leadership behavior(s) that can be sharpened to help you overcome it.

Busyness

It was his first day on the job and John, the new CEO, was a bit nervous as he prepared to meet with his leadership team. He had a number of questions he wanted to ask and was looking forward to learning from the group.

Once everyone was seated around the table, John explained that he would be asking the team one crucial question during each of their meetings over the next few weeks. Their answers would tell him more about their leadership than anything else he could think of. Then he posed his first question: "How visible are you in the work environment?"

There was silence as eyebrows rose and people looked around at each other. Finally, Rita spoke up: "John, it's a fairly small office. We generally see most of our colleagues in the parking lot coming in the building each morning or at the coffee pot." Chip added, "People see us come and go between meetings; there are conference rooms on each floor." Rita continued, "Besides, with all due respect, we are very busy people and catching our staff when we can is the best we are able to do. I think it's all that's expected of us, really."

"I see," said John, smiling. "Rita, tomorrow I would like you to accompany me as I make the rounds of our accounting department."

The next day, as the two leaders visited the area, they saw a large box sitting on a table with a sign that said, "Books for Kids." Curious, John approached the closest employee, pointed to the box, and asked, "What is this all about?" Blushing, she said, "Sir, every fall I ask people in my department to donate a used or new book for a child. Then I take these to a local elementary school whose students have no money to purchase material to read outside of the classroom. The teachers divvy up the books and reward their students with them."

"Ah . . . what a wonderful project. I have several books I would like to contribute," replied the CEO. "Thank you for your commitment to helping others."

He turned to Rita. "I would like to start a company-wide program to recognize staff like Martha who model our values. I'd appreciate your input about who would be the best person to make a reward and recognition program a reality."

"I can see it would be a good idea," she replied, "I will have some suggestions to you first thing in the morning."

John and Rita continued rounding for the next 30 minutes. As they started toward the elevator, she asked, "What will be the next question you have to ask our leadership group?"

John smiled. "All in due time."

In today's world, we tend to have a "check the box" kind of existence. We are expected to fulfill one obligation after another, whether at work or in our personal environment. Multitasking is the new management survival skill, and as a result, we feel there is no time to make relationship-building connections with our co-workers. "Git 'er done" seems to be the rule of the day. Building relationships falls by the wayside.

If you are a leader who is so blinded by a perpetual state of being busy that you have no time for visibility in the work environment or for making connections, consider reassessing the ability to *organize* and *prioritize*. These are the attributes that enable you to drill down into your schedule and find time for an everyday presence in the midst of your staff. Taking control of the calendar calls for personal involvement, rather than allowing an assistant to pencil in every hour of the day for you. It must be a priority to connect with people as they go about their daily tasks. How else will you uncover examples of employees who have an impact on the lives of others in very special ways?

What is your schedule like today, tomorrow, and next week? Is there room on it to do the things critical to your ability to flourish as a human being? If not, how will you find the time to recognize ordinary greatness when it touches your day or that of someone close to you?

Self Assessment: Busyness

- Do you visit work areas on a consistent basis to establish relationships with your colleagues and open lines of communication?
- Do your colleagues consider you to be approachable?
- Is your daily work a check-the-box kind of existence, consumed with doing tasks rather than being available for others?
- Are you addicted to schedules and calendars that leave limited room for personal connections?

Preconceived Notions and Compartmentalization

As the management team filed into their next meeting with the new CEO, John greeted everyone warmly. They saw that the projection screen had been pulled down, and John had his laptop open in front of him.

He opened the meeting with, "As you will recall, I announced that each time we get together over the next few weeks, I will be asking you one question. Oh by the way, did everyone get my e-mail about the children's book donation program Rita and I discovered as we rounded last week, and the new recognition program we are instituting?"

As murmurs of assent were heard, John looked pleased. "The question I have today is: How do we get discretionary effort from our employees?"

"If you mean how do we get more work from our staff, then I am all ears," commented Carl.

"Oh that's an easy one," Bill replied. "Bonuses. People like money—and we have a good bonus program here."

"Absolutely," agreed Paul. "Money makes the world go 'round and makes everyone work harder. I make sure my people get their annual bump in pay."

"John," said Todd. "Surely you know that plant ops won't respond to anything else. Occasionally when the grumbles get loud enough, I put another bonus program in place—that's what they understand."

"Really?" replied John. "Anyone else have something to contribute?"

When no one replied, John continued, "I don't think we are on the same page when talking about discretionary effort. Let me ask you another question. How do you know that your people consistently contribute their maximum because you offer some kind of monetary incentive?"

"Um . . . everyone knows that." replied Bill "Come on, John, don't tell me that you won't work harder when you know there is a bonus on the line—or a good raise?"

"Sure, I like money as much as anyone else," replied the CEO. "But it's not what causes me to make a commitment to do my very best. As a matter of fact, I don't think it is necessarily what makes your colleagues go above and beyond either."

He fired up his laptop. "Here are the results of a survey I conducted in my previous job. When I asked employees to list the factors that cause them to get fully engaged in the work they do, it became evident where money really falls in the pecking order. Their results are very similar to data from other sources of research I've seen."

The group watched as a PowerPoint slide came into view on the screen. Here is what they saw:

I am engaged because . . .
1. I know the importance of my job to the success of the organization.
2. I am recognized for my contributions.
3. My company invests in developing me.
4. My work environment and colleagues are supportive.
5. I am fairly rewarded financially.
6. I have the resources to do my job effectively.
7. My work is fulfilling and achievable.

(continued)

"You will notice," said John, "that money is ranked fifth in terms of importance. What is most remarkable, however, is the role each of us plays in engaging others to tap into their discretionary effort. The bottom line is that we, as leaders, are responsible for whether or not our staff brings its full commitment and effort to work every day."

As he closed down his computer, the team looked at one another in surprised silence. Finally, Rita spoke up. "Well, John, I believe I speak for all of us when I say that we are certainly looking forward to the question you will bring to our next meeting . . . or perhaps I should say the answer."

Perhaps you harbor preconceived notions about what motivates the people you lead, or maybe you tend to compartmentalize when it comes to what individuals are capable of achieving. If you are prone to these blinders, you will find yourself overlooking ordinary people who have risen above adversity, have prevailed regardless of setbacks, or have achieved high distinction in spite of a limited background. Finally, rest assured that the heroes who walk among us are not motivated by money.

Concentrating on the leadership attributes of *communication* and *people development* will help you remove these two blinders. Communication is strategic to the discretionary effort that contributes to greatness in the work environment. Ensure that each and every person understands the impact of their efforts on the success of the organization—that they are, in effect, owners responsible for exceeding your expectations. Connect the dots for employees between what they are doing and the value they bring to the organization.

Communication is also about the ability to listen. Opening your eyes to greatness includes hearing about it. Tune in to the feedback that will help you identify those who are going above and beyond and, in doing so, making a huge impact on someone's life.

The leader's role is to teach, coach, and inspire others to be the best they can be. Motivate and challenge colleagues to high performance;

help them stretch beyond preconceived capabilities. When you develop an employee, you not only create a star achiever capable of greatness; you build the organization's bench strength as well.

In addition, developing people and bringing out latent greatness is richly served by knowing what motivates them. The experts tell us the desire to realize personal potential, to be self-fulfilled, drives us in ways that nothing else can—not money, prestige, status, achievements, or titles. Those who demonstrate ordinary greatness have reached this highest and greatest plateau of self-actualization; perhaps it is their intrinsic source of motivation.

Self Assessment: Preconceived Notions

- Do you know what motivates your staff?
- Are you hesitant to support new ways of approaching workplace issues?
- Are you supportive of everyone, regardless of their current level of performance?
- Do you believe certain people will never exhibit high performance?

Self-Assessment: Compartmentalization

- Are you able to link what employees do on a daily basis to the success of the organization?
- Do you believe that an individual's discretionary effort directly reflects their level of commitment?
- Do you encourage staff development and foster participation in learning opportunities?
- Is it difficult for you to envision an employee working outside their area of expertise?

While the word "bias" carries a negative connotation, in reality it simply means that personal opinion is slanted in a particular way. All of us can be favorably or unfavorably biased toward certain people, situations, and outcomes. Often, we do not even realize the bias because of our innate spatial blindness. It takes proactive work to overcome this blinder and ensure that those who follow us are supported in every way.

Personal Bias

The team sat anxiously waiting for John to enter the room. The last two weeks had been interesting, to say the least. They were beginning to realize John was bringing a new perspective on leading, and that he had discovered extraordinary people and events that the team had never noticed.

John walked in and was quick to begin the meeting. "Let's start with the question today, actually two questions in one. First, how many of you have heard of spatial blindness? And second, what do you do to ensure that spatial blindness isn't limiting the potential of those you lead?"

Bill was the first to speak up. "I remember spatial blindness from my psychology class in graduate school. It means we see the part, not the whole. We kind of assume everyone is just like us, and we don't stop to consider others' perspectives."

"Correct, Bill," replied John. "And what would be the logical outcome of spatial blindness?"

"Well, our 'take' on people might be incorrect or limited because we fail to see the big picture? And we might not be as empathetic as we could be?"

"Good answers. Now for the second part of the question— how do you make sure you are not holding people back from their potential because of this limitation?"

The leaders looked at one another. "Wow, that's a tough one, John," Carl finally replied. "I'm sure we've all been guilty of this at one time or another. What are your thoughts?"

"Spatial blindness is common in business relationships," John replied. "And I admit that I used to be guilty of this. In my former leadership position, I had no trouble seeing my own world, but it wasn't easy for me to see the work environment as my employees experienced it. It was easy for me to feel the pulls and tasks that faced me daily, but not those that staff went through. I had some preconceived ideas of their jobs, but not really a full understanding and appreciation. Similarly, my spatial blindness made me pigeonhole people and their capability. I failed to empower others because I didn't believe in their ability to succeed at critical tasks."

"Then one day everything changed."

The room grew quieter as everyone leaned forward in anticipation.

John continued. "One of my colleagues brought me an idea that I first scoffed at. I told him leaders wouldn't go for it, and I thought it was a waste of time. But he kept at me and finally convinced me.

"It was a job-shadowing program for our leadership team. All leaders had to actually work in a front-line role for a day alongside a colleague from that particular area. They had to wear the appropriate uniform and perform the actual tasks. In essence, they had to meet the challenges head-on that those in the trenches face every single day.

"What an eye-opener! I shadowed one of our housekeeping attendants at the hotel and let me tell you, that is some tough work. The sights and smells and physical demands are very difficult to handle. And all the rooms need to be cleaned within a certain timeframe, so the pressure is tough. Yet this lady kept a steady pace and a smile on her face the whole time. We never passed a person in the hallway that she didn't welcome to the hotel and ask about their stay in the city.

"As we approached a particular guest room, she told me about the couple staying there. She had met them the day before as they were leaving for a sightseeing tour. The couple was celebrating their 50th anniversary with the trip they had dreamed about for years. They told her they had made a promise to each other on their wedding day that they would celebrate their 50th wedding anniversary in San Francisco. The couple's story was even more touching, as the wife had shared

(continued)

that she had cancer and most likely had less than a year to live. Kathy, the housekeeper, was touched by the story and told her supervisor. When the couple returned from their day of touring, they found a bottle of champagne waiting for them, compliments of the hotel. That's when I realized that my worldview, so to speak, was off. This employee was a valuable asset to the organization and an inspiration to her co-workers. What else was I missing? How much had my selective perception, my bias, blinded me to the potential for greatness in other staff? And what could I do about it?"

The room was silent as he finished his story. Rob, the chief learning officer (CLO), cleared his throat. "So the first step would be to investigate what it would take to put a leadership job shadowing program in place here?"

"It would be a beginning," John replied. "But just a beginning—we have a long way to go."

To ensure you are not spatially blind to greatness or the potential for it, you should concentrate on two leadership core competencies— being *team-oriented* and developing *personal mastery*.

Most leaders will tell you that teamwork is essential for success, yet they often fail to let true teamwork shine through. Ask yourself whether you are surrounded with people who think differently than you or if you gravitate toward putting together a team of those who are quick to support your opinions.

Work outcomes are greatly enhanced by team diversity because of the variety of perspectives, problem-solving methods, and idea exchange. It becomes much easier to have eyes "wide open" to potential and to recognize the extraordinary things that co-workers do both on the job and in their personal lives. However, it is a different matter if the work environment is peopled with those who think alike and who prefer the safe and secure way of doing things.

The best leaders also practice teamwork through empathy. When you are driven to understand and appreciate the opinions of others, to view the world through their eyes, it is very hard to be biased. When you can relate to, feel for, and have insight into your team members, it becomes much easier to put aside spatial blindness. Your ability to lead and work well with others often depends on your capacity to "read" them. This is achieved by consciously imagining what it must be like to see things from others' points of view.

You can also develop your empathic abilities by taking the time to ask questions of your team, listen carefully to the answers, and use your imagination to view the world through their eyes. Lacking empathy is a slippery slope to all sorts of bias that will impact your ability to lead effectively.

Personal mastery calls for the self-confidence to ensure everyone's potential is fully realized, regardless of the position they hold in your organization. You realize your strengths and involve others who possess the strong points you lack. The best leaders practice self-development. They read books to learn how others encourage greatness and see its potential in people.

One of the most famous readers in American history was President Abraham Lincoln. His love of books and reading shaped his life and the world. There was only one book in the Lincoln family cabin—the Bible—so young Abe read it. He also borrowed classics such as *Aesop's Fables, Pilgrim's Progress,* and *Robinson Crusoe.* When the noon break came after he had worked in the fields all morning, he would pull a book from his pocket and throw himself down under a tree to read. When he was about 22, he decided to improve his grammar. He walked six miles to obtain the loan of a grammar book, which he studied by firelight. And later, as a Congressman in Washington, D.C., he would bury himself in the Library of Congress to read, much to his colleagues' amusement.

We know what this great man accomplished in his abbreviated time on earth; perhaps there is no better example of a leader who refused to be constrained by preconceived notions, compartmentalizing, and personal bias. Had his thinking and humanistic perceptions not been shaped by the knowledge he gained from reading the world's most profound books, where would we be today in this nation?

Reading helps us see the world as it truly is and remove blinders. It helps keep faulty information at bay, enlarges our immediate world, and makes it far more possible to recognize the great deeds that ordinary people are doing all around us, every day.

Self Assessment: Personal Bias

- Do you get your impression of the work environment from firsthand experience, instead of what people tell you?
- Is your opinion of others influenced by what you hear?
- Are you quick to jump to conclusions based on your previous experiences?
- Does the ability to relate to others' ideas and opinions come easily to you?

External Focus

The announcement that the next meeting would be held in a new location—the organization's coffee shop—caught everyone a bit off guard. Filing into the sunny shop at the appointed time, the team gathered around small round tables and waited for John to arrive. Cheerful servers brought out carafes of fresh coffee and tea and placed baskets of warm muffins on each table. Everyone enjoyed the chance to relax and visit for a few minutes as the servers carefully poured hot drinks and offered cream and sugar.

When John arrived a few minutes later, he was offered his choice of beverage and a muffin by a beaming server. He accepted both, thanked the server quietly, greeted the team, and invited them to join him in a conference room located just down the hall from the coffee shop.

"I'm sure you're wondering if we're playing some sort of game," John remarked with a grin.

"Well, it's certainly a relaxing way to start a meeting," Rita responded. "We know you well enough by now to know you've got something on your mind."

"What did you notice about the coffee shop?" John asked.

"The coffee was hot," Bill said.

"The muffins were fresh," Rita added. "And the tables were clean."

"Well, they probably knew we were coming and spiffed up the place," Carl said.

"No, I can promise you didn't get any sort of special treatment," John said. "Anything else you noticed?"

"I'm guessing there's something we missed," said Bill.

"Did you notice anything in particular about the people serving you?"

The team glanced at each other.

"Ummm . . . they were young?"

"Yes."

"They were cheerful?"

"True."

"Wait—I think I remember hearing something about this from my daughter," Todd said. "They're from the local high school, aren't they? It's some kind of internship thing they're doing for credit?"

"They are from the high school, and they are getting credit, and they're also getting paid," said John. He picked up a remote, pressed a button, and the wall-mounted monitor lit up. The team watched as a news story began to play.

"This week we're focusing on a special group of high school students," the reporter said. "Linda Barton's class of exceptional students from Eagle Bay High School is getting some real world business experience at a local coffee shop." The report described how students with special needs were thriving under the work responsibilities and the encouraging supervision of people from their school and from the organization.

At the end of the clip, the room was quiet for a few seconds.

"How do you suppose these kids would fare in a typical interview setting?" John asked.

"They'd probably have a tough time selling themselves," Carl said.

(continued)

"It would depend on the position they were applying for," Bill said. "I mean, we do have policies in place for making sure everyone is considered equally here."

"Well, you can see how they're working at the top of their abilities," Rob said. "It's a win-win situation for them and for us, right?"

"But would you have hired them without seeing the news story?" John probed. "Despite our policies, is it possible that we let our perceptions predict the performance we expect from other people?"

"Well, we're surrounded by packaging and marketing at every turn," said Bill. "In fact, it's a consideration for every one of us in this room—what our image is, how to strengthen it, how to maintain what's good, and how to improve what's lacking."

"Exactly right," agreed Todd. "I think the coffee shop is a great example of the importance of looking beyond the packaging to see the potential."

We talked about the blinder of external focus in Chapter 3. Another example of this blinder and its power over our thinking is the first impression. A mere six- or seven-second glance at a person and we have decided how we feel about the individual. We have passed judgment courtesy of physical appearance, facial expression, clothing, body language, and other instinctual signals of which we are not even aware! In the book *Blink*, author Malcolm Gladwell created a whole new term for this: *thin slicing*.[2] An expression that has actually become part of mainstream lexicon, it refers to using limited information as the basis of a conclusion about a person or situation. However, this largely subconscious phenomenon has a distinct downside: thin slicing is easily corrupted by our likes and dislikes, prejudices and stereotypes, experiences and knowledge.

The Kennedy-Nixon Presidential debates of 1960 were the precursor of thin slicing. The "Great Debates," which marked television's grand entry into presidential politics, afforded viewers their first-ever opportunity to see the candidates vie competitively. Yet it was not the content of their speeches that determined who won. Instead, the visual element skewed the validity of the outcome. Nixon, who had recently spent two weeks in a hospital recovering from a serious knee injury, appeared thin and gaunt. Wearing an ill-fitting shirt, he refused the makeup that would have improved his pallor and perpetual five-o'clock shadow. In great contrast, Kennedy, who was expensively attired, looked tan and fit, confident, and well-rested.

In the debate's actual substance, the two were equally matched. Those who listened to it on the radio actually proclaimed Nixon the winner. However, on the television stage, Nixon's sickly appearance and demeanor were no contest for Kennedy's youthful looks, projected air of privilege, and charisma. The television audience focused on what they saw, not what they heard. Afterward, studies revealed that viewers considered Kennedy the winner of the first debate by a large margin.[3] Lesson learned: Television sells the vision; it is up to us to interpret the greatness.

In the next chapter, we will explore the characteristics of organizations that promote ordinary greatness. By adhering to the philosophy and practices suggested, any business can develop an environment that encourages ordinary individuals to achieve quiet acts of selfless greatness.

Blinders prevent leaders from recognizing and fostering ordinary greatness.

- When was the last time you observed a leader who failed to see greatness, and which blinder was present?
- What impact would removing the busyness blinder have on your ability to observe ordinary greatness?
- What do you do to avoid the tendency to judge people based on a first impression?

Chapter 5

Characteristics of Ordinary Greatness

I'm surprised at the number of people who don't pay attention at all, as if I'm invisible. Because, you know what, I'm makin' a lot of noise.

—Violinist Joshua Bell, in the *Washington Post* article "Pearls Before Breakfast"[1]

O rganizational blinders like corporate practices, policies, and expectations (culture) can either guide or derail the organization's cultivation of ordinary greatness. If an organization's leaders can be compared to a musical conductor, the organization's culture is the musical score. While leaders set the tone, an organization's culture is a barometer of how clearly ordinary greatness is identified, celebrated, and encouraged. Effective leaders keep a keen ear tuned to their organization's distinct and dynamic culture. In turn, the ways that leaders lead affect an organization's alignment—how the workforce functions on a day-to-day basis and how invested the workforce is in the organization's success. The organization's alignment determines how—or whether—the parts and pieces of the organization function smoothly together to achieve its goals.

Impact of Culture on Greatness

An organization's culture is the sum of its shared values, beliefs, philosophies, ideologies, assumptions, attitudes, and norms, which knit the organizational members together. The culture is responsible for the ingrained thoughts and behaviors that occur with little reflection or consideration. Culture is "the way we do things around here"—the habits and expectations that define the essence of the organization and how people act and interact within its domain. The culture determines whether it is more important to please the customer or the boss; who gets promoted and why; what behaviors are valued in the organization; and whether ordinary greatness is identified and celebrated.

Are you happy with the current culture of your organization and the context it provides for the workforce? Does your culture encourage your employees to do great things? Is your culture yielding the results you desire, or is it limiting your potential?

Every organization has a culture. Unfortunately, many, if not most, cultures develop by happenstance. They are the result of a myriad of actions, experiences, decisions, and personalities that determine, over a period of time, how people think and behave while at work. Successful organizations do not leave their culture to chance. They deploy mechanisms to evaluate the current workplace and then strategically plan for the changes that need to take place. A culture that promotes ordinary greatness must be carefully cultivated, monitored, and supported on an ongoing basis. Cultures that embrace ordinary greatness are associated with higher employee engagement, higher productivity, better talent retention, and innovative approaches to issues and challenges.

Most, if not all, organizations are internally aligned to produce the results they get. Are the expectations geared for mediocre work that merely allows the company to stay in business and show a slight profit? Is the environment one where an act of ordinary greatness seldom takes place and probably would not be recognized if it did? Or are leaders and employees expected to excel and be co-owners of a thriving company? The expectations for high performance are entrenched, and employees quietly and selflessly fulfill a vision of greatness.

An atmosphere of discovery and appreciation for the extraordinary things that occur on an everyday basis is a vital part of a great organizational culture. Unless an organization has the processes, practices and systems in place to identify and celebrate greatness, it rarely if ever happens.

We recently worked with a client company that had been experiencing declining results for several years. After assessing the organization's processes and practices, we met with the leadership team to review the results. During the course of the meeting, it became clear from the comments, body language, and apparent lack of ownership that the leadership team was disengaged. To better understand their perspective, and more importantly to demonstrate the impact they were having on the workforce, we scheduled a follow-up session. During the session, we gathered perceptions of the current culture and helped participants identify what needed to happen to bring about change.

Each leader was given a "sticky" notepad and asked to write a word describing the current culture on each sheet and then post them on the wall. The 40 leaders generated over 200 words. As leadership gathered in front of the postings to survey the words, gasps were heard. Comments included, "This is horrible," and "There is little that is positive represented here." One person, with tears in her eyes, commented, "I am crushed to see these words associated with my organization." Out of more than 200 postings, less than 20 sticky notes could be considered positive—friendly and caring. The rest were words such as *fear, unfair, punitive, uninspiring, boring,* and *stuck.* Next, we asked the leaders to identify the cultural attributes that were missing from their organization, but would lead them to greater success. The words they envisioned that would indicate the existence of a culture of ordinary greatness—including visionary, celebrates, participatory, innovative, develops people, communicates—were missing.

The tough part of this exercise was telling the participants that the words they posted on the wall reflected their leadership. It was obvious their attitudes about the organization had permeated the entire work environment. It was also obvious that their very actions supported the negativism they now faced. This vicious cycle continued to promote the declining results.

The good news was that because the exercise reflected their leadership, they had the opportunity to improve the organization's culture through their attitudes and actions. The work that followed involved selecting the top attributes in three categories: (1) positive ones they wished to sustain; (2) negative ones they wished to eliminate; and (3) desirable ones they wanted to develop within the organization. The entire leadership team committed to a set of organizational strategies as well as specific leadership behaviors that would support a healthier culture. The work of the team is represented in Exhibits 5.1 and 5.2.

Within six months, the listing of attributes had significantly improved, and the workforce was beginning to feel more engaged and empowered to do great things. Why not try the exercise with your own organization in mind?

- What are the first three words that come to mind that describe your current culture?
- What are three attributes that are missing from your culture that would lead to greater success?

Finally, a word on the need to assess your organization's culture periodically: Forward-thinking companies do not get caught off-guard by undesirable attributes that sneak into their workplace culture. Nor do

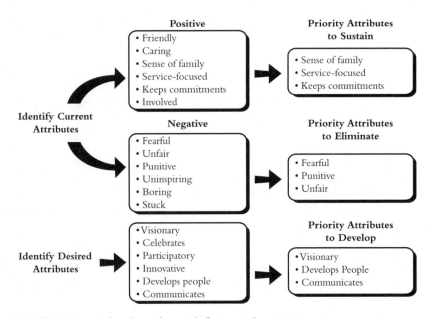

Exhibit 5.1   Cultural attributes: defining and prioritizing

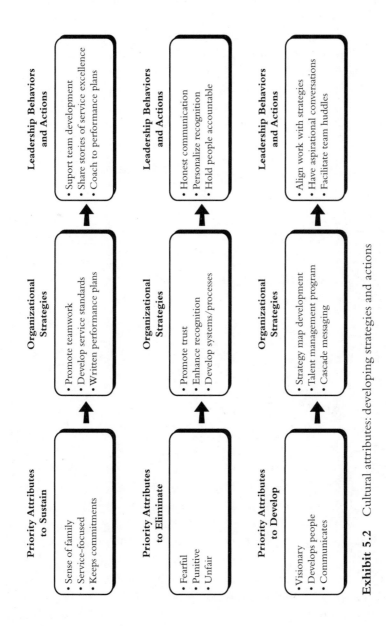

Priority Attributes to Sustain
- Sense of family
- Service-focused
- Keeps commitments

Organizational Strategies
- Promote teamwork
- Develop service standards
- Written performance plans

Leadership Behaviors and Actions
- Suport team development
- Share stories of service excellence
- Coach to performance plans

Priority Attributes to Eliminate
- Fearful
- Punitive
- Unfair

Organizational Strategies
- Promote trust
- Enhance recognition
- Develop systems/processes

Leadership Behaviors and Actions
- Honest communication
- Personalize recognition
- Hold people accountable

Priority Attributes to Develop
- Visionary
- Develops people
- Communicates

Organizational Strategies
- Strategy map development
- Talent management program
- Cascade messaging

Leadership Behaviors and Actions
- Align work with strategies
- Have aspirational conversations
- Facilitate team huddles

Exhibit 5.2   Cultural attributes: developing strategies and actions

organizations become irrelevant because they have not identified new attributes necessary to be successful in changing times. We recommend that an organization conduct a "culture audit" at least every five years to assess the work environment. The audit should focus on the prevailing attitudes of employees, the characteristics for which the company is known, and how customers are treated. In addition, consider how the company is planning for and responding to marketplace challenges.

Importance of Alignment

In Chapter 3, we identified one of the most common blinders to greatness as the setting itself: it happens in a place where it is least expected. An important reason most commuters in the Metro station missed the greatness of Joshua Bell performing right in front of them was that they entered the station expecting the same experience they had every day. *The Washington Post's* experiment threw them for a loop. In a Metro station was a concert violinist—an experience not in line with their expectations. The misalignment of the two meant most of the commuters reacted by failing to recognize the prominent superiority of this artist. They trusted their expectations and cast aside the unexpected opportunity to discover, recognize, and appreciate greatness.

What is alignment? Taking what has been previously disconnected and finding relevance in the whole. In the business world, alignment is so central to success that lack of it is the top issue facing most companies. Alignment is critical in ensuring that organizational cultures support the concept of ordinary greatness. Everyone is working hard— "making noise," as Joshua Bell described his efforts—but a focused and consistent approach is missing. Teamwork, goal setting, and even day-to-day work are misaligned and working at odds to one another. There is no harmony or concert of activity. Patrick Lencioni, author of *Five Dysfunctions of a Team,* likens this to a golf team whose members play individually, only to tally everyone's scores at the end of each round as the group's score. They are playing golf, but they are hardly doing it as a team and certainly not concerned about the whole.[2] Contrast that analogy with the story of the English gentleman walking the streets of

London one morning when he happened upon three workers laying stone. Curious about what they were building, he approached the first worker, tapped him on the shoulder and asked, "What are you doing?" The worker barely looked up as he slapped more mortar down saying, "You must be blind if you can't see I'm laying stone." Undeterred, the gentleman approached the second worker and inquired about what he was working on. The second mason had little more to say, "Can't you see that I am building a wall?" Determined to learn what was going on, the gentleman tapped the third worker and asked him what he was doing. This time the worker stopped, stepped away from the wall and, wiping his hands off, said, "Why, I'm on the team that's building the new cathedral." Whatever the cathedral in your organization, does every person know how his or her part fits into the whole? Fred Smith, chairman of Federal Express, said, "Alignment is the essence of management."[3] Management is about aligning people and systems to create high performance and produce results. Consider the illustration shown in Exhibit 5.3.

The top portion provides a sense of how a misaligned organization goes about its work, while the bottom portion speaks to a fully aligned, high functioning organization. Just by viewing the illustration, the vast difference between the two organizations becomes apparent. The top portion represents a piece of music that simply cannot be played effectively, no matter how talented the musicians or extraordinary the instruments. It's just a collection of scrambled notes with no apparent tune or composition. By contrast, the bottom portion is a selection from

Exhibit 5.3   Misalignment and alignment

the piece played by Joshua Bell in the Metro station: "Chaconne," from Johann Sebastian Bach's *Partita No. 2 in D Minor.*[4] Even though the score looks complicated and was composed around 1720, a musician with the right training and experience can quickly gather the information needed in order to play the piece just as the composer intended.

Misaligned organizations miss out on extraordinary people, events, and opportunities. They simply fail to see and capitalize on what is occurring throughout the organization each and every day. Lebovitz and Rosansky, authors of *The Power of Alignment: How Great Companies Stay Centered and Accomplish Extraordinary Things,*[5] liken misaligned organizations to cars out of alignment. The travel can be bumpy, and serious problems are sure to develop if the situation is not corrected quickly. Proof of this statement appears in business news and in the popular culture. Some examples: Radio Shack lays off workers by e-mail; auto executives agree to contract with labor unions for benefit packages they cannot possibly provide; and a current television series, *The Office*, owes at least some of its popularity to viewers saying "I can identify; this is my office!" at the end of each absurd episode. Remember, we are perfectly aligned to produce the results we get.

Characteristics of Organizations Aligned for Ordinary Greatness

Organizations that successfully align themselves for greatness share four common characteristics: (1) clarity, (2) claim of ownership, (3) committed communication, and (4) connectivity via systems and processes. Each of these provides a critical link to the alignment of the organization as a whole. Individually, they are essential. Collectively, their presence or absence provides valuable clues about an organization's condition and its future.

Clarity

Remember the Cheshire Cat from *Alice in Wonderland?* His words of wisdom seem prophetic: "If you don't know where you are going, any road will get you there." A study reported in *Industry Week* revealed that only one-third of employees are fully engaged and know their employers' mission.[6] The survey revealed that the main reason employees are disengaged is their employers' failure to communicate organizational strategies. Successful organizations provide clarity that connects people and their work to meaningful goals and the strategies of the organization. Does every person in your company know what the most important thing is for your company this year? This month? This week? Today?

In 1951, Florence Chadwick was the first woman to swim the English Channel both ways. On July 4, 1952, she attempted to swim the 26 miles between Catalina Island and the California coastline. On this particular day, the water was ice cold, and the fog was so thick she could hardly see the boats that flanked her on both sides. She swam for hours as Americans watched on television and as her coach and mother encouraged her from the support boats. After 15 hours, 55 minutes she indicated she could not make it and asked to be pulled from the water. Only when she was in the boat did she discover she had stopped just one mile from her destination.

When interviewed by reporters, Chadwick said, "Look, I'm not excusing myself, but if I could have seen land, I could have made it." The fog had prevented her from seeing her goal. Two months later, Chadwick attempted the swim again. As before, the fog was thick and prevented her from seeing the California coastline. But this time, she made it. She credits her success with keeping a mental image of the coastline in her mind as she swam. She had to clearly visualize her goal to successfully complete the swim.[7]

Claim of Ownership

Claim of ownership is a commitment from an individual to view the organization as if he or she owned it. Would employees in your organization act any differently if they actually owned the business and were spending their own money? For a quick self-assessment of one's tendency to behave as an owner, we often ask seminar audiences to silently respond to two questions (1) When you finished your shower this morning, did you hang the hotel towel up or leave it on the floor? (2) When you finish your shower at home, do you hang your towel up or leave it on the floor? They get the point. Ownership means actively looking out for the company's best interests and its bottom line. When money is spent, it may not come from employees' personal bank accounts, but there is no doubt that the financial health of an organization has an impact on the financial health of its employees. We once heard a client express it this way: "If you wouldn't find enough value or return to spend your own money on something, then don't spend the company's money on it." Taking ownership means that if I hear about it, suspect it, see it, overhear it, should have seen it, or just know about it, I OWN it.

One of our favorite slides to use in training sessions is a photo of road kill face down in the middle of the road with two yellow stripes painted down its body with the caption, "It's not my job." When beginning work with new clients, we often ask employees to tell us the most common excuses for not getting things done or for lack of results. As trite as it may sound, the most frequent excuse we hear is, "It's not my job." Ownership is about making it your job regardless of what the job description outlines. It means picking up every piece of trash on the floor like you would in your own home. It means walking a customer to their destination instead of pointing the way. It means owning the customer experience so that no one walks out of your doors unsatisfied with the service they received—even if you were not the point of contact for the customer. We all make decisions about how much we are willing to commit to an organization. The most successful organizations are the ones that have figured out that employee ownership is the magic ingredient that can propel an organization to success.

Committed Communication

Feeling "in the loop" generates commitment and energy throughout the workforce. Jan Carlson said, "An individual without information cannot take responsibility; an individual who is given information cannot help but take responsibility."[8] Misalignment is almost always accompanied by a communication barrier. More often than not, finger-pointing is a hallmark of any conversation about lack of communication. Take this real-life example: A primary complaint among employees of a large corporation was that they frequently learned about happenings and events in the company from reading the local newspaper. A primary complaint from the executive leadership team was that employees would not take ownership. The question we posed to executive leadership: "Take ownership of what? They don't know what is going on." The executive leadership team took on the challenge to enhance communication across the organization. They began to practice management by walking around: they ate lunch in the cafeteria, included written updates in the employee newsletter, and hosted all-hands meetings of the entire organization every quarter. Within six months, not only did communication rank higher on the employee opinion survey, overall morale had made a significant gain.

Connectivity via Systems and Processes

Often leaders suggest employees are at fault for missed deadlines, lackluster results, or low morale. While that may be true in many instances, before judgment can be passed, the leader must examine the systems and processes that dictate how the work gets done. It could be that broken systems and misaligned processes are the culprit. The easiest way to discover barriers is to ask employees, "What is getting in the way of you doing the best job you could possibly do?" We once facilitated a session with more than 500 leaders to uncover outdated, ineffective, and duplicated practices and processes within the organization. When this team of leaders sat down to consider the task, they rose to the occasion and identified more than 50 practices that were outdated, more than 75 processes that were ineffective, and 25 practices and processes that were duplicated. They even identified six monthly reports that absolutely no one read! By making changes based on this input, the organization estimates they were able to save over $2 million a year.

Organizational Practices that Create Misalignment

Earlier in this chapter, we discussed the importance of alignment and identified the characteristics of organizations that successfully align themselves for greatness. Through our work with hundreds of organizations, we have also identified some of the most common "people practices" that create misalignment.

Repeatedly Relying on the Same People, versus Considering Others Who Are Ready for New Challenges

While we certainly believe that the 80/20 rule applies in most organizations and human endeavors (80% of the results come from 20% of the people), we also believe that the 80/20 rule leaves a lot on the table when talking about the potential of human capital. Unfortunately, most leaders rely on a select few to carry the weight of the project or the department. The same people are continuously asked to serve on committees and take the lead on projects. These "tried and true" individuals have captured the attention of the leader. As a CEO client once said, "If you want something done, give it to the busiest person on the team." There is a reason some people are busier than others—they get things done! We were once employees of a firm where there was a wide disparity in productivity and expectations. The productive few were often called upon to "save the day." That approach bred two cultures: (1) high performance and (2) mediocrity.

What if leaders were to take a different view of this misaligned behavior? What if they stopped relying on the same select few any time results were needed? We suggest you look at your team's workload and consider how well it is dispersed among the team members. Have some people been working so long on the same projects that boredom has surely set in? Perhaps the people sitting on the sidelines are anxious for an opportunity to contribute. What are you doing to develop the chance for them to shine and make a meaningful contribution? A true commitment to these ordinary greatness principles requires a resolve to lead differently. Your leadership effectiveness will best be measured by the results your staff produces.

How people are promoted to new positions is one of the mysteries that continues to fascinate us as we work with organizations seeking a higher level of performance. Actually, one of the first questions we ask new clients is how people move up in the organization. Their response tells volumes about the organization's culture. Take out a piece of paper and list the last three people in your organization who received a promotion. Now, beside each name, list the known and expected reasons for the promotion. Point made. We are familiar with one well-known healthcare system whose administrator embodied the mediocre performance of his organization. To the astonishment of many, he was promoted to a system-level position, not based on skills and qualifications, but because he happened to be positioned for the promotion. Over time the entire system became known for the same mediocre results—no big surprise!

One of the most disappointing trends we see in organizations is a lack of any type of formal succession planning. Most organizations do not understand the long-term impact of talent management systems or even how to replace talented individuals. Instead, promotions go to the people who are best known (remember the most popular kid on the block?); or those with whom the boss is most comfortable playing golf; or (horrors!) those who "brown-nose" the best. An organization we once worked with had clear directions for promotions within the company—go to the boss, play to his ego, and you were selected. However, when a business spends focused time creating strategic talent management processes, that organization always sees the investment returned, usually many times over, in terms of a strong and well-developed leadership team.

A critical element of leading people is understanding fit. Jim Collins calls it "the right people in the right seats on the right bus." He goes further in saying "if you have the right people on the bus, the problem of how to motivate and manage people largely goes away."[9] When everyone on the team is doing what each does best, the group can then concentrate on results with fewer distractions.

We began consulting because as veterans of corporate America, we became disgusted by the cookie-cutter approaches taken by most talent managers, human resource professionals, and (yes) most consultants. "This is how I manage, and you had better adapt!" is the prevalent attitude.

Take a moment to consider a parent with three children, ages two years, eight years, and fourteen years. Would this parent use the same parenting skills with all three kids? Not successfully, they would not. Now, we are not suggesting that leaders treat their subordinates like children. But as we studied greatness in leaders, we found the ones who got the best results treated people differently based on that person's skill set, experience, talents, and worldview. Of course, this required that each leader actually get to know their staff members as people. The truly great leaders become almost obsessed with fit—hiring for it, managing it, and also understanding that fit sometimes causes poor performance.

We are reminded of an old story about a Siamese cat who was fortunate enough to live with his wealthy owner in an ornate mansion at the top of a hill. Rumor was that this cat drank his water out of a sterling silver dish and had all of his meals served to him by a butler! The custom in this house was that the owner would arrive home from work every evening, have dinner and then retire to the study where he would sit by the fire, read a book, and stroke the cat's fur. There was just one problem: every night the owner would stroke the cat's fur, only to rub it the wrong way, tail to neck, greatly annoying the animal. One day the cat could take it no more and decided to leave. He ran away down the hill to the town below where he met an alley cat who, recognizing him, asked the cat, "Hey, are you that cat who lives in the house up on the hill? I heard you drink your water from a sterling silver dish and that you have all your meals served to you by a butler. Is that true? Yes? Then what are you doing down here?"

"I ran away!"

"Why?"

"I have my reasons."

"Tell me."

"Well, every night my owner would come home, sit by the fire, and rub my fur, and I hated this."

"Why?"

"He rubbed me the wrong way."

When he heard this, the alley cat started laughing. "You idiot, you did not have to run away! You just had to turn around."

When your employees are struggling, could it be due to fit? If so, you might not have to fire anyone—if the job is rubbing them and you the wrong way, can you turn around your ideas and views of what the job should look like? Can you be more open to new ways of job design and fit? For example, a hopeless introvert would probably not be a good fit for front office reception, but might enjoy data entry. People with a strong intuitive inclination on the Myers-Briggs Type Indicator find detail work exhausting, but might be better at sales or relationship-building ventures.

Celebrating the "Lone Genius" versus Effectively Delegating Responsibilities

We often use Russian stacking dolls to make our point about the lone genius. As dolls are opened, each subsequent doll becomes smaller and smaller. Such is the case of the self-focused, lone genius. As this individual works within the context of self-sufficiency, there is little or no sharing of expertise, and certainly no building the skill base of others. Thus the overall expertise, knowledge, and skill diminish with each new colleague, impacting the organization's ability to leverage its intellectual capital. The concept of the stacking dolls is also true in hiring new staff. Noted advertising executive David Ogilvy states it well: "If each leader hires someone less than himself, we will be a company of very small people. If each hires someone greater than himself, we will be a company of giants."[10]

A corollary to the lone genius is lack of delegation. This takes a number of forms, one of which is the idea of "if you want something done right, do it yourself." A frequent complaint and frustration of most executives is *"I'm too busy!"*—too busy to coach employees, too busy to role model the right behaviors, too busy to spot ordinary greatness. So they often ask us for help: "How can I be more effective and have more time to do the important things?" Well, when we observe their typical day, we find they are often doing things that should be done by subordinates. One of the first effectiveness strategies we coach busy executives to implement is the simple act of not attending meetings where their direct reports are in attendance. Obvious exceptions to this would be a staff meeting that the leader called, or a one-on-one meeting with team members.

Now, this seems easy enough, but very few executives we know have mastered this task. To be the leader you need to be, to have the time to see and develop ordinary greatness, you must evaluate every task and ask yourself, "Can this be done by someone else?" If the answer is yes, give it up. Spend your time doing the things only you can do. The payoff will be greater development of staff, less frantic days, and the achievement of recognizing ordinary, everyday greatness.

Failure to Track and Measure the Important Things

At the end of this year, CEOs will stand up before their boards, executive colleagues, and employees to deliver a message something like this: "The numbers weren't what they should have been this year. We didn't make budget. Our customer service scores declined, and employee morale took a hit. But *it was a great year!*"

What? By whose measure was it a great year? As consultants, we are always startled by the number of executives who, at the end of contractual engagements, ask us, "How did we do?" In reality, they should not have to ask. The results reveal the answer. When it comes to the leadership development and training industry, for instance, it seems like the wrong things are consistently being measured. The emphasis tends to focus on how many people attended the training (we lovingly refer to this as the "butts in seats" measurement), whether they enjoyed themselves, if the room temperature was acceptable, and how they liked the lunch that was served. No one actually checked to see if they *learned* anything! No one checked to determine whether the training led to measurable results. Marshall Goldsmith, author of dozens of books on leadership development said it best:

> A lot of what passes for leadership development in companies can be a waste of time. See if you recognize this process. Your company taps you as a future leader. It sends you to "leadership camp," which can last anywhere from a day to a couple of weeks. You're entertained by a parade of speakers (like me), and afterward you're required to critique the speakers and rate how effective they were. If the company is particularly rigorous about gathering information, you may be asked to critique the hotel and the food. But nobody is critiquing you. Nobody is following up to see what you learned or if you have actually become a more effective leader. As a result, the people who may be learning (and changing) the most are the speakers, the hotel staff members, and the cooks.[11]

If you want the right answers, start by asking the right questions. We recommend every leader select just a few key measures to track throughout the year. Set a numerical goal in each of these areas. Then over-communicate these to staff, and monitor and report progress constantly.

Sales and production numbers, customer service ratings, employee turnover, and quality indicators are a few important measures of an organization's success. To supplement those, consider some additional measures that support the concept of ordinary greatness:

- Number of development hours provided to staff
- Number of ideas and improvement suggestions submitted by staff
- Percentage of staff attending communication briefings
- Percentage of time leaders spend being visible in the organization
- Number of thank-you notes to staff from leaders each week
- Number of front-line staff involved on teams and committees

Consider the primary school classroom full of rambunctious children. Even the most talented teacher must juggle attention in many different directions. Usually the attention goes to the most aggressive child reinforcing the exact behavior the teacher is trying to stop. So it is in organizations whose leaders tolerate un-called-for behavior by simply working around certain individuals.

What's true in the classroom is also true in the boardroom, and beyond. We know of an organization that employs an individual known far and wide for his negative attitude. Tom worked in the hospital's maintenance department, and most people in the organization made it a point to stay away from him. Not only did he wear a constant scowl on his face, he rarely had a kind word to say to anyone. One day, Tom was called to a patient's room to repair a sink that had a continuous drip. As Tom entered the room, he grumbled an unrecognizable greeting to the patient that indicated he was not too happy about getting the repair call. Within a few minutes, Tom approached the patient's bed accusing her of stripping the faucet by turning the handle too hard and proceeded to give her a stern lecture about being careful with the hospital's property. Little did Tom know this patient was suffering from end-stage cancer and was so weak that not only could she not walk unassisted, she certainly could not apply enough pressure to strip the sink's faucet. Later in the day, the patient shared her conversation with Tom with the attending nurse and apologized for any problem she had caused. She said the nursing staff had been so good to her and she did not want to be a bother to anyone at the hospital. The nurse could tell the patient felt bad about the interaction, even though she had not caused the situation. The nurse gently told the patient that Tom "had issues" along with a bad attitude, and that everyone at the hospital just tended to ignore his inappropriate comments and behaviors.

Do you have Toms in your organization who are getting attention for inappropriate behaviors? Did his behavior move the organization toward its goal of 99% customer satisfaction? What would happen if suddenly Tom was not getting the awareness he desired? Remember, what you permit, you promote!

While working in a call center whose focus was customer service, Lynn quickly discovered the focus was on the clock, not necessarily on the customer. During peak call times, representatives were encouraged to meet a quota of solving at least five problems per hour and instructed to keep phone conversations as brief as possible. Daily notices were circulated around the office naming "top performers." Reminders were sent when phone calls exceeded ten minutes in length. When one representative was singled out for recognition because she consistently "made quota," others noted the consequence of her speed: her customers had to call back again when their problem was not resolved correctly. This did not do much for morale in the office, and customers frequently commented that while the company's product was excellent, its customer service was deplorable. What would have happened if the customers had been given priority over the clock?

Lack of Transparency

Have you ever left a meeting knowing the most important things were not discussed? This seems to be a basic tenet of modern corporate life—not discussing the important things, despite spending countless hours in meetings. Instead, we discuss these items during the "meeting after the meeting." Perhaps this is because people feel safer sharing opinions when the boss is not around to pass judgment. Consider this statement by Jerry Hirshberg, President of Nissan Design International, Inc.:

> Many of the best ideas are communicated through whispers— in the hallway meetings that happen after the official meeting. That's because people worry about how the boss will react if they speak the truth. What's remarkable, of course, is that these whispered ideas are what companies are most hungry for.[12]

People are looking for leaders who can build an environment of no secrets where the truth can be spoken, leaders who are authentic and transparent. Why is there a dearth of this kind of leadership? A number of reasons—some individuals are fearful of being truly transparent ("if they know what I know, I will not have power over them anymore."). Others have never truly learned how, or have seen an incorrect role model ("Do as I say, not as I do."). And there are some who just do not care about the culture and are fairly miserable at work ("I am just trying to get through the day.").

An organizational culture that promotes ordinary greatness must be carefully cultivated, monitored, and supported. Leaders who embrace this opportunity are the key to ensuring a culture supportive of ordinary greatness. It becomes the leadership brand of the organization.

Eliminating organizational blinders requires that leaders understand the impact of culture and the importance of alignment.

- When was the last time you challenged the notion that "It has always been done that way?"
- What have you done lately to support a healthy culture at your organization?
- How do you consistently connect the parts and pieces of the organization's work in a way that is meaningful to your subordinates?

Chapter 6

Creating the Context for Ordinary Greatness

"I don't think that if he's really good, he's going to go unnoticed. He'd get a larger audience in Europe . . . but, okay, out of 1,000 people, my guess is there might be 35 or 40 who will recognize the quality for what it is. Maybe 75 to 100 will stop and spend some time listening."

So, a crowd would gather?

"Oh, yes."

And how much will he make?

"About $150."

—EXCERPT FROM INTERVIEW WITH LEONARD SLATKIN,
MUSIC DIRECTOR OF THE NATIONAL SYMPHONY ORCHESTRA,
ON WHAT MIGHT HAPPEN IF ONE OF THE WORLD'S GREAT
VIOLINISTS PERFORMED INCOGNITO BEFORE A TRAVELING
RUSH-HOUR AUDIENCE, AS QUOTED IN *THE WASHINGTON POST*[1]

An article in the *Harvard Business Review*[2] posed a startling question that continues to capture our attention. As the authors of this article addressed what it takes to be a leader who inspires others to achieve extraordinary results, we wondered how those being led would respond to the following scenario: Suppose you were invited to select a boss who would be able to bring out the best in others. What characteristics would you look for? We talked with front-line employees from many different types of businesses. We consistently heard comments such as "a leader who is there for us, is available when needed," "someone who listens to us," "a person who asks for our input and lets us be part of making decisions," "someone who appreciates me and the work I do," and "a leader who helps me grow."

Those we interviewed were optimistic in the belief that their leaders have the opportunity and capacity to promote ordinary greatness in the workforce and that their leader has the potential for personal "greatness." They were clear in their belief that the opportunity lies with the attitude and behaviors exhibited by leaders on a daily basis. They were also quite adamant about the fact that greatness is associated with the personal impact leaders have on others. One fundamental difference we found in our interviews with front-line staff and our interviews with leaders: Leaders tend to associate greatness more with accomplishments, achievements, and business results, and less on the impact they have on others. This kind of thinking is contrary to the adage, "You define the success of a leader by the success of that leader's followers."[3]

Shawn is a leader who has worked for many employers, some of whom were able to spot ordinary greatness, and some who could not. He told us, "One boss I had made everything about him. I mean, it was almost like he thought we existed to serve him. And it did not take long for staff to realize this—and you know what? They started to leave. And, of course, the best people left first, because they had options. Another leader I worked for was the exact opposite. In subtle ways, he always made sure you felt better about your work at the end of the day than you did when you started. And it was not like he did not challenge you. In fact, he probably pushed me more than anyone else in my career, but every day was memorable."[4]

We asked leaders a series of questions, requesting that they stand up after each question if they could respond in the affirmative. This activity was inspired by management guru and former chairman and CEO of General Electric Jack Welch. The results are quite telling.

- How many of you would identify yourselves as people of high integrity? *Of course, the entire room stands.*
- Now, how many of you have conducted a performance evaluation in which you failed to give employees honest, unvarnished feedback about exactly where they stood in your eyes? *Naturally, the entire room sits back down.*
- Are you really a person of high integrity if you do not tell the truth and do not seek common understanding with your staff regarding expectations and commitment levels?

This is one of the reasons we do not see ordinary greatness. We do not find common ground with others regarding what greatness looks like, often because we are concerned with preserving the feelings and comfort levels of staff. However, keeping staff comfortable is not the role of a leader. As we heard from Shawn, in his experience, the most challenging leader was the most positive and had the greatest impact. Our friend Clay Sherman, author of *Gold Standard Management: The Key to High Performance Hospitals*, is fond of saying, "Letting you stay in your comfort zone could be the most cold-blooded management move of all. Caring management does what works and gets results, which keeps the organization alive and provides you with a job."[5]

If you are really concerned about and interested in the lives of your staff, you will tell them the truth, with lots of kindness and positivity. The rule of "five positives for every negative" is a good guideline to follow in providing balanced feedback that is truthful yet encouraging. Jack Welch says, "You simply do not have the right to call yourself a manager if you are not regularly telling your people what they are doing well and how they need to improve."[6]

As we examined the leadership characteristics mentioned in the research we conducted, and considered our experiences with thousands of leaders, it became clear that leadership behaviors that drive greatness in others can be discussed in three realms, as shown in Exhibit 6.1: (1) leadership that sets the context for ordinary greatness; (2) leadership that promotes employee engagement; and (3) leadership that cultivates the potential of the workforce.

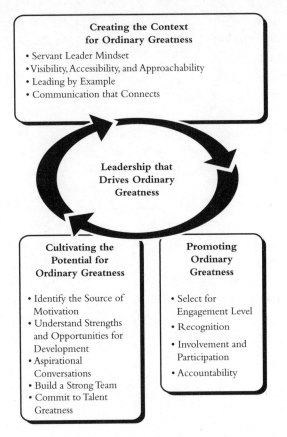

Exhibit 6.1 Leadership that drives ordinary greatness

Leaders set the context for recognizing, developing, and leveraging everyday greatness. Leaders must ensure that the environment is one that encourages everyone to work to the best of their abilities. That process starts with building relationships, a primary function of those serving in a leadership role. Life is about relationships, and success in the workplace is intricately tied to the personal connections that are built and maintained. Self-help author Brian Tracy said, "The glue that holds all relationships together—including the relationship between the leader and the led—is trust, and trust is based on integrity."[7] Establishing trust is the most basic requirement of any relationship. Without it, all else falters.

We were reminded of this caveat as we observed a new leader forge ahead in a division of high achievers. His mistakes were many, and his blindness to his inability to engage others and to build trust was astounding; needless to say, the results were devastating.

The classic mistakes that many new leaders make were compounded as we observed his style over the first 90 days—he discounted everything, and I mean everything, his colleagues had developed and achieved through years of hard effort. There was a constant, demeaning stream of negative comments about how the work of the division was being conducted. If the practices and processes were not being done in a way he had done them in the past, they were wrong. There was no opportunity for others to offer insight into why the various tools and methods were developed and how they supported the organization's objectives. He was acutely unaware of the consequences of many of his decisions. There was only a declaration that everything was going to change—to his way of doing things.

Changes began taking place in a vacuum. There was no communication, which resulted in a constant state of anxiety, nervous tension, and rumors. Those we spoke with were so unsettled they could not focus on their work, and were having clear-cut symptoms of profound stress.

Collaboration with his colleagues to engage them in making the changes never happened. Dictates were the order of the day. People who had labored long hours because of their commitment to the business began leaving at 5:00 P.M. sharp. Many made a habit of "working from home" to avoid interaction with this leader. Office potluck lunches, once an occasion for camaraderie, ceased to exist as people preferred to "lay low."

Perhaps this leader's most devastating behavior was the pitting of staff against staff as a tactic, in his mind at least, that would create loyalty to his leadership. Confidential information, even information on who he was thinking of firing, was shared with a selected few who became his "go-to" people. A strategic plan was developed without input and presented to the team as a final product with no opportunity for reaction or feedback.

By the fifth month of his leadership, six of his best performers had resigned and those remaining were actively searching for a way to get out. It is not surprising that this division did a quick downward spiral and has little chance of surviving.

This leader had a lot of great ideas that could have had a tremendous positive impact on the organization. This is a story of the failure of leadership. We see it all too often as we work with organizations across the country. If, instead, this leader had focused on creating the context for ordinary greatness, the story would have been much different. Four specific strategies will be discussed: the importance of a servant leader mindset; the impact of visibility, accessibility, and approachability; the necessity of leading by example; and the practice of communicating in a way that connects with the workforce.

Servant Leader Mindset

Setting the context for ordinary greatness begins with a mindset that leaders are there to serve their subordinates. Understanding the concept that "to lead, you must serve" is central to providing a work environment that sets itself up for promoting greatness among its individuals. A great deal has been written about servant leadership in recent years, yet the concept is thousands of years old and can be found in the 600 B.C. strategic treatise by Chinese sage Lao Tzu, *The Tao Te Ching*.

> The great leader forgets himself
>
> And attends to the development of others.
>
> Good leaders support excellent workers.
>
> Great leaders support the bottom ten percent.
>
> Great leaders know that
>
> The diamond in the rough
>
> Is always found "in the rough."[8]

It is about taking the best of who you are and connecting with the best of those you serve. Unlike hierarchical styles of leadership, servant leadership emphasizes collaboration, trust, empathy, and the ethical use of power. The very essence of the servant leadership philosophy is that the individual is a servant first, who has made the decision to lead as a way to serve others, not to enhance their own circumstances or increase their power. To us, servant leadership also means that leaders have faith in their people, believing that everyone has the capacity for greatness and that they can be trusted to do great things.

Effective leaders demonstrate their commitment to servant leadership by their day-to-day decisions and actions. Often these actions are subtle and done without fanfare or attention. Some of the more obvious actions that demonstrate servant leadership might include organization-wide celebrations in which leaders cook and serve pancakes or hamburgers to staff; hosting events for staff and families in the leader's home; walking staff to their cars in the evenings; attending sporting events of the children of staff; and sending birthday cards to the children of staff.

The story of explorer Ernest Shackleton is an excellent example of leadership with a servant's heart. What kind of leader places this type of "help wanted" ad?

"Men wanted for hazardous journey. Small wages. Bitter cold. Long months of complete darkness. Constant danger. Safe return doubtful. Honour and recognition in case of success."

In 1915, Shackleton's ship, the *Endurance,* was trapped in ice floes in the frigid Weddell Sea deep in the Antarctic. The ship's crew could hear the ice freezing around them. By September, grinding icebergs had crushed the ship's hull, leaving Shackleton and his men stranded on a vast ice sheet 1,000 miles from the nearest inhabited land.

Shackleton sustained morale and created a unified team by keeping everyone busy—and equal. For example, during the long months in which the crew lived on the *Endurance* as a winter station, Shackleton ignored the predominant class system of the time and had scientists scrubbing floors alongside seaman and university professors eating beside Yorkshire fisherman.

In addition, Shackleton encouraged more than work-based camaraderie. The men played football on the ice, participated in nightly singalongs and toasts to loved ones back home, organized highly competitive dog-sled races—and even collectively shaved their heads, posing for expedition photographer Frank Hurley.

In the face of changing circumstances and constant danger, Shackleton remained positive and decisive, which buoyed his crew. Further, throughout the 22-month *Endurance* expedition, Shackleton was able to bring out the best in each of his men.

Shackleton's extraordinary leadership skills contributed to his 27-man crew successfully surviving the nearly two years they were stranded in the Antarctic.[9]

Visibility, Accessibility, and Approachability

Texas oil and gas entrepreneur T. Boone Pickens said, "There are many ways to avoid mistakes, but the best way to sidestep the disasters is to be available. You don't have to make every decision, but you should always be accessible. If your people are smart, they will keep you informed, and if you're informed, you're part of the decision. With that in place, it's easy for you to back your people, and that eliminates second guessing."[10]

We agree with Pickens. The best way for leaders to develop relationships throughout the organization is to have a high level of visibility and interaction with employees. Perhaps no organization embraces these concepts more than the Toyota Motor Corporation. Deeply embedded within the culture is the philosophy of *genchi genbutsu*, translated as "go and see."[11] Leadership at all levels believes in going to the source to find the facts to make the right decisions, build consensus, and achieve goals.

The benefits of visibility:

- Builds trust between staff and management
- Provides opportunities for the leader to identify and recognize ordinary greatness occurring during the course of the workday
- Lets staff know that you care about the work that is being done and appreciate its importance to achieving organizational goals
- Encourages staff to make suggestions and offer opinions to improve the organization creating a stronger sense of ownership
- Provides the context for identifying opportunities for improvement and understanding the dynamics of decision choices
- Helps the leader recognize obstacles or barriers that need to be removed to achieve better outcomes

However, the myriad benefits of visibility are often lost on executives. For example, recently we worked with a healthcare organization in a small midwestern community. The primary issue we were asked to address was a lack of employee engagement, leading to low overall productivity. To acquaint ourselves with the organization, we asked the CEO if we could accompany him on his daily rounds. We were surprised to learn that he did not routinely do rounds but preferred to work from his office. Nonetheless, we embarked on a rounding expedition. Starting on the fifth floor we were greeted by several nurses who gladly paraded us around the unit, explaining the specialty services they offered and the current day's patient load. This was repeated on the subsequent floors, each team a bit surprised to see us in their domain. In fact, the first words out of one nurse manager's mouth when she saw us were, "Is something wrong?" It was evident that the CEO, even with 15 years' tenure at the organization, was not known well by his staff. This became even more apparent during our final stop, food services. Walking through the door, the CEO wished everyone a good morning. An older worker (we found out later that she had worked at the organization 27 years) asked the question in the back of everyone's mind: "Who are you?" The CEO replied by stating his name. The next question from this feisty food services worker was, "And what do you do around here?" Speaks volumes about the disconnect between this executive leader and his staff.

I (Brian) was recently coaching a leader who had to give the following feedback to his boss, the company CEO: "I need to let you know that last week, while I was out of the office, my staff paged me with an urgent message telling me that a state inspector had arrived unannounced, and that I had better get there soon to host this important inspector. I raced back to the office, and when I arrived and met the inspector, I realized that the inspector was you. The staff did not know you, had never seen you, and mistook you for an out-of-town inspector." Fortunately, that was a wake-up call for the CEO to improve his visibility, accessibility, and approachability.

While the most effective visibility is personal, there are countless ways that leaders can enhance their visibility when they are unable to be there in person. In a former job where I traveled constantly, I (Pam) used to send a postcard to the office staff from each new city I visited as a way to bring them into the work I was doing. We know of one executive who sets a stack of 20 notecards on her desk at the beginning of each week. She never leaves the office for the weekend unless all 20 of the notes have been written and mailed.

Another way for leaders to be visible is through a powerful but rarely used strategy called *managing up*. Simply put, managing up is the ability to bring a leader into the conversation or meeting without their physical presence. It is a way to indicate to staff that senior leaders are aware of their efforts, appreciate their work, and want to hear their ideas and suggestions. After all, everyone wants the big boss to know they are contributing to the success of the company. For example, Sherry is facilitating the monthly meeting of her sales department. During the review of results accomplished during the previous month, she shares the following: "I spoke with Jim (senior executive to whom she reports) and he wanted to make sure that I passed along his kudos for the record month. He mentioned that he does not recall achieving such high sales numbers in more than five years and that he appreciates all the hard work he knows went into getting these results." Through Sherry's efforts to manage up, she was able to make a connection between the staff and their senior leader, and to reinforce the senior leadership's awareness and appreciation for the day-to-day work and accomplishments of the staff.

Leading by Example

Nothing develops or destroys trust and confidence in leadership more quickly than the observable behaviors of leadership. Role-modeling the organizational values and expected behaviors are critical to creating an environment of consistency. Actor Will Rogers said, "People's minds are changed through observation, not argument." It is simple: people do what they see being done. Leaders must be aware that they are "on stage" at all times and that others are taking their cues from the behaviors they observe. A leader who arrives at meetings late is giving permission for others to be late. A leader who parks in the customer-allocated spaces sends a message that it's okay to park there, even if the personnel manual notes otherwise.

I (Pam) had an opportunity to see ordinary greatness in action. We have all read accounts of airplanes stuck on the runway for hours while passengers nervously contemplate their missed connections. One cold February morning I was on such a flight from Atlanta to Newark when the pilot's voice came over the intercom to announce there had been a ground stop for all outgoing traffic until further notice. I waited for the onslaught of complaints from the passengers and the turmoil that would result from the announcement. Instead, the pilot came out of the cockpit to personally deliver the details about the delay, after which he invited questions from the passengers and patiently responded to each and every query. He continued to offer frequent updates over the next several hours, even at times conveying the message that he had no idea what was occurring. Then, to my astonishment, he walked down the aisle several more times throughout the long wait, asking passengers, "Are you doing okay?" "Is there anything we can do for you?" Finally, he invited all the kids on board to join him in the cockpit for a "flying" lesson.

Captain Chris Waples of Delta Airlines seized the opportunity to do something great in the face of adversity. He took a less-than-ideal situation, put himself in his passengers' shoes, and treated them the way he would want to be treated under similar circumstances. By putting everyone on the same "team" and setting a positive example, he minimized the potential stresses among his passengers.

Occasionally, leadership needs to make a bold statement through their behavior to demonstrate their commitment to the principles they espouse. At one of our client sites, the following exchange occurred between Brian and the senior leadership team:

Brian: You have hired me to advise you on ways you can be more effective and engage your staff. Good news! I have found a relatively easy, inexpensive way. I understand that due to construction onsite, every morning, employees are required to drive to a lot five miles from headquarters, park their cars, and ride a shuttle bus to headquarters. This process is repeated in reverse every evening. Needless to say, it is not very popular with staff, but it is made worse by the fact that none of you ride the shuttle bus. In fact, I noticed that you all have individual private parking spaces right by the front door.

CFO: But we have to—we have early meetings and are in and out all day. Besides, would that really make a difference, our riding the shuttle bus?

Brian: I believe it would. Give it a try. It would model servant leadership, you would have a captive audience for communication, and, hey, carpooling saves gas.

CEO: (joking) Can we have our own shuttle bus? (Laughter)

Brian: Well, that is not what I was talking about, but give it a try—people will notice.

There was some grumbling, and when I left, I wasn't sure they were going to invite me back. They seemed very disturbed by the suggestion they should ride the shuttle bus.

Well, later in the week, I started getting voicemail messages from members of the executive team stating that they had started riding the shuttle bus, with two results: There was quite a buzz around the workplace, and they felt better about being connected with staff in this new way. Positive peer pressure being the power that it is, it was not long before all members of the team were riding the shuttle bus. In fact, those parking spots at the front of headquarters that the executive team used were reassigned to employees with high ratings from customers based on regular surveys.

Later, when we commissioned a before-and-after survey of staff, the item that was most frequently referenced by staff in the open feedback/written comments section was the fact that senior leadership was riding the shuttle bus every day—more than pay raises or any other environmental factors.

Communication That Connects

Stephen R. Covey, author of *The 8th Habit,* asserts that the difference between the actual contribution of an individual and their potential greatness has a solution. "One word expresses the pathway to greatness—voice. Those on this path find their voice and inspire others to find theirs. The rest never do."[12] He believes that the crucial challenge of leadership today is communicating in a way that connects, inspires, and supports employees. We saw this play out in the 2008 presidential campaigns, as the political commentators wrote about each of the candidates "finding a voice." It was at that moment, the commentators felt, that the candidate truly connected with the voters. It is a powerful engagement strategy.

Think about all the various pieces of communication you receive each day. Between meetings, conversations, newsletters, e-mails, and television, each of us receives an overwhelming amount of information every day. To deal with it, we selectively screen or filter what does not speak to our current interests and needs. To break through this veritable fortress, leaders must communicate in a way that is timely, understandable, meaningful, and inspirational.

Earlier, we identified lack of communication as a primary source of dissatisfaction for employees. The issue is exacerbated by common faulty assumptions made when communicating. Leaders are caught in the trap of thinking "We spoke, you heard." Even more dysfunctional is when leaders are caught in the trap of thinking "We spoke, you heard, you did." In their book *The Leader's Voice*, authors Crossland and Clarke state that at its best, leadership communication "establishes understanding, invites agreement, encourages and enables a willingness to act, and creates a path for action."[13]

The 1995 movie *The American President* is a film written by Aaron Sorkin about a fictitious U.S. president, the travails of his personal life, and the inner workings of his position. The exchange below is between Lewis Rothschild, one of the President's advisors and speechwriters (played by Michael J. Fox), and President Andrew Shepherd (played by Michael Douglas):

Lewis Rothschild: People want leadership. And in the absence of genuine leadership, they will listen to anyone who steps up to the microphone. They want leadership, Mr. President. They're so thirsty for it, they'll crawl through the desert toward a mirage, and when they discover there's no water, they'll drink the sand.

President Andrew Shepherd: Lewis, we've had Presidents who were beloved who couldn't find a coherent sentence with two hands and a flashlight. People don't drink the sand 'cause they're thirsty. They drink the sand 'cause they don't know the difference.[14]

Drinking the sand has detrimental effects on organizations. One thing that causes people to drink the sand is a lack of clear measures of success. In the absence of clear measures, people in the organization will focus on something. That *something* could be what you want them to focus on, ideally things like goal achievement, leadership development, and personal improvement. Or, they might drink the sand instead, focusing on petty rivalries, confusion, and turf building. They do not do this because they are bad people. They do this because they *do not know the difference*!

Management guru Peter Drucker noted, "Where organizations fall down is when they have to guess at what the boss is working at, and they invariably guess wrong."[15] If you asked your staff, "What is the most important thing we are working on right now?" or "What key results are we aiming for this year?" right now, would they know or would they have to guess? Would they drink the sand of a mirage or the clear, cold water of an oasis? You determine that by your actions and your communication.

Eliminate guessing and position yourself for success in spotting and developing ordinary greatness by creating clarity. Establish clear measures of success, overcommunicate those measures, and track them maniacally. Remember, if people have to guess, they will guess wrong.

"Leadership is fundamentally about how we relate to others, how we engage, mobilize, focus, and ignite each other," says Omar Khan, author of the book *Liberating Passion: How the World's Best Global Leaders Produce Winning Results.* "Passionate people are hired into most leading companies. Within three months, however, the passion is often gone. Companies are 'passion castrators' in many ways." Khan states the single greatest passion killer is poor communication.[16]

With that in mind, we consistently recommend three proven communication strategies to our clients: team huddles, cascade messaging, and storytelling. All are interactive exchanges between leaders and employees that go beyond mere information sharing.

Team Huddles

We are used to seeing team huddles on the football field. During huddle time, the team quickly assesses the situation and prepares each team member for the play ahead. Perhaps the most obvious place you might see a team huddle in the workplace is in a restaurant, right before opening its doors for the day. The wait staff gathers and learns the daily specials, VIP reservations, and scheduled events. The disbursement of this information is fast, easy, and consistent, and allows the opportunity for questions, clarification, and discussion. The huddle concept works for sports teams, restaurants, and any business that employs more than one person.

I (Pam) had an opportunity to experience a huddle at the corporate headquarters of the Ritz Carlton hotel chain a number of years ago. I found myself in a meeting with a dozen Ritz Carlton executives reviewing a set of policies. Suddenly a young lady at the table stood up and said, "It's time." Everyone seemed to know what to do, except me. But being a quick learner, I did what the others did —filed into the elevator and exited on the third floor. Once there it became apparent that the expectation was to join the others who were lined up in the hallway. Taking my place, it was just seconds before the then-CEO, Horst Schulze, emerged from his office and took a spot along the wall. He opened his suit jacket, pulled out a sheet a paper and began reading a message—the same message that was being delivered through huddles at all the Ritz Carlton properties across the world that day. The message that day had to do with how employees should respond to hotel guests who have had too much to drink. It was informative! After the message, Mr. Schulze announced the winners of the previous day's potluck. He handed out gift certificates for best casserole, best dessert, and most innovative dish. He ended the meeting with a reminder of the company's slogan, "We are ladies and gentlemen serving ladies and gentlemen. Have a great day." Within 12 minutes, my group was seated back in the conference room and continuing our discussion on policies and procedures. I had just been part of the Ritz Carlton's "Line-Up," a communication process used to send a consistent message to a diverse employee population across the world that sets and reinforces the culture of that organization, every day!

Huddles or "check-in" meetings result in greater cohesion, improved communication, and more efficiency, as many issues can be resolved in these short, frequent gatherings. Most important, meeting on a daily basis gives you the opportunity to articulate the most important things the team should be working on—this will ensure alignment of expectations and accountability. Stories shared during the huddle allow you to learn about extraordinary things happening in the organization. This helps drive recognition of high-performing employees who are on their way to greatness.

The most effective huddles are held at a regularly scheduled time and last no longer than ten to fifteen minutes. The meeting is conducted while everyone is standing, to reinforce the goal of brevity. This type of format works well for huddles:

- Urgent issues
- General updates
- Expected challenges for the day
- Educational message tied to the organization's values, standards of behavior, etc.
- Discussion question
- Recognitions
- Inspirational quote for the day

Team huddles also encourage esprit de corps and collaboration among team members. For instance, Janet worked for several years at an organization that used team huddles to deploy consistent messaging over geographically dispersed office locations. She participated in a daily ten-minute team huddle. Eventually Janet's husband was transferred and they moved to another state. Within three months, Janet was diagnosed with an aggressive form of cancer and found herself in a strange new city where she knew no one. Once she had successfully completed treatment, she wrote in a letter to the CEO of her former company, "I truly did not know what I was going to do when I was first diagnosed with breast cancer. It was the support and encouragement of my former colleagues that got me through this personal crisis. They were incredible with the notes, gifts, and calls of encouragement. As I think back to my time there, I realize that our team bonded because of the time we spent together in our daily huddles. Those ten minutes each morning where we devoted ourselves to the team and focused on the work ahead made all the difference in the world. I believe it was the most important thing we did and was responsible for the extraordinary results we were able to achieve. More so, the time together created lifelong friendships that I will cherish forever.

No matter what changes may occur in the future, please keep the team huddles going strong—you never know who will need the support and the encouragement next."

Our clients have also found that the daily huddles often negate the need for weekly or monthly sit-down meetings. The frequency and the formatted agenda provide real-time information, so issues and challenges can be addressed more quickly. By including a brief educational message, daily huddles account for 40 hours of training and development each year. Staff members become more engaged and experience an enhanced sense of ownership because they are empowered by knowledge. It is a great way to reinforce an organization's values, its attitude toward customer service, and its approach to being colleagues.

Cascade Messaging

Remember the game once played as children sitting in a circle with one person whispering a sentence that is then whispered to the next person and so on until the last person receives the message? When the last person shares what they heard with the group, the final message is typically nothing like the first message. So it is with organizational communication. As messages are passed along or "cascaded" through the organization, via different leaders with different styles and different interpretations, the original message becomes convoluted.

One of the most common organizational communication issues we see is how leaders convey information. For instance, after attending a monthly management meeting, leaders share the highlights with their staff all in the name of transparency—a good thing. However, it is highly possible that each leader in the room heard the information differently and drew their own conclusions about which highlights should be shared with staff. Each leader goes out with the best intentions about sharing, but the messages are different and often conflicting, creating misalignment in communication. An effective practice we have observed is the inclusion of a final item on the agenda of the management meeting that reviews in very specific terms the key messages that should be cascaded once the leaders leave the room. Before everyone leaves the meeting, there must be clarity on the messaging to be shared and a commitment to the agreed-upon action steps.

We recommend that each cascade communication be put through a four-step filter to ensure its relevance and its ability to connect with the intended audience.

- *Message.* What are the key points that need to be communicated? How does the message connect to the interests and needs of the recipients?
- *Media.* What venues can be used to get the message out?
- *Managerial Effort.* What is the role of leadership in the cascade messaging effort?
- *Repetitive Messaging.* How will the message be reinforced?

Storytelling

Storytelling is an easy-to-use tool that is available to all leaders, yet it is seldom used. Even though people seem to remember stories longer and with greater recall than they do facts and figures, many leaders are hesitant to tell stories to their staff. Here are some of the reasons given for not using storytelling:

- *I am not good at it.* Keep trying! You are probably a better communicator than you think you are, and stories are our best friends because they are often well-received and appreciated by staff.
- *I do not want to seem phony.* Then be sincere. People can tell whether you are being genuine or manipulative.
- *I don't have any good stories.* It may be because you are not looking. Every day, look for examples of staff doing the right thing, then share these stories with staff.
- *It seems too touchy-feely for me.* Storytelling can be fun without being syrupy or fake. In difficult times, a leader cannot afford to pass up any free tool such as storytelling.

When done well, storytelling has the following benefits:

- Storytelling serves as a communication tool for you to help share ordinary greatness. If leaders use only one form of communication exclusively, staff will become bored and begin to tune out the leader. When staff tunes you out, you are less likely to be able to spot ordinary greatness in their lives and in their work.

- Storytelling is one of the best forms of training. If you wish to train staff to display greatness, tell them stories of how others have done this. Give staff something they can relate to and emulate.
- Storytelling inspires. Nearly everyone has heard a story of someone practicing ordinary greatness that has inspired them to do likewise. This is why every healthy culture has heroes, and why we have museums dedicated to the greatness of political leaders, inventors, soldiers, and others who did great things. These temples to storytelling serve to keep the story alive and also allow us to dedicate time to apply lessons learned from the past to the present.

Storytelling empowers. When people hear stories of how others have overcome blinders to achieve ordinary greatness, they start to think, "Hey, I can do that, too." While working with an urgent care center in the western United States, we heard that the administration had encouraged staff to do "whatever it takes" to please the customer. This was put to the test one night when a man with chest pains drove himself to the center. He was ultimately rushed to the hospital. There was one catch: When he had checked in, his beloved dog was in the car, and he was very concerned about the dog. The care center staff remembered the "whatever it takes" mantra, and they kenneled the dog at the center's expense until the dog's owner was safely out of the hospital and home. The administration was thrilled, as was the customer. For a few hundred dollars, the center now had a happy customer who was out in the community saying great things about the center, including writing a positive letter to the editor of the local newspaper. (Old advertising adage: "There's publicity you pay for, and then there's publicity you pray for." This publicity was definitely the latter.) So this story of the dog was told to all the hospital staff as an example of "whatever it takes."

A few weeks later, on a different shift, a man who was driving through the city on the interstate with his family was having trouble breathing, and the entire family showed up at the center with him. Again, he had to be admitted to the hospital for tests, and his family was in a difficult spot—out-of-town with no funds to afford a hotel. Staff remembered the story of the dog being kenneled and said, "Well, if we can put up a dog, I'm sure we can put up people!" They then found a reasonably-priced hotel room for the family and billed it to the center with their manager's permission. This solution led to more accolades for the center, as well as a tighter connection with the community. Lives were touched, staff was more engaged because they were able to make a difference, and it all began as a story. Reinforce ordinary greatness behaviors by telling stories.

Leaders must ensure that their organization's environment supports each person to be the best they can be.

- What have you done to lay the foundation for a work environment that creates enthusiasm and passion?
- Do you "connect" with staff when you communicate?
- What is the impression that your colleagues have of your interactions over the past week?

Chapter 7

Promoting Ordinary Greatness

Playing the violin looks all-consuming, mentally and physically, but Bell says that for him the mechanics of it are partly second nature, cemented by practice and muscle memory. . . . What he's mostly thinking about as he plays, Bell says, is capturing emotion as a narrative: "When you play a violin piece, you are a storyteller, and you're telling a story."

—Excerpt from "Pearls Before Breakfast,"
The Washington Post, April 7, 2007[1]

Employee engagement results from leadership that is engaged. When executives ask us, "How do we get our employees more motivated, engaged, and committed?" we are reminded of the words of Edgar Powell, known for his ability to design team-building activities: "No organization is stronger than the quality of its leadership."[2] The executives' question begs another question: "How motivated, engaged, and committed are the leaders of this organization?" Some executive teams understand, and some do not get the connection between the two. But the connection is real, and it is strong. It has to be for leaders to truly understand the difference that a fully engaged workforce can make. We will focus on four key strategies that leaders can use to successfully engage their staff: select for engagement level, recognition, involvement and participation, and accountability.

Select an Engagement Level that Promotes Ordinary Greatness

Leaders can set themselves up for success by paying close attention to the hiring process. A leader can do all the right things, avoid blinders, recognize greatness, and remain open to spotting ordinary greatness in staff, but if the hiring process recruits and hires staff who do not buy into the need to be great and who do not exhibit the attitude needed to be great for customers and co-workers, nothing else will really matter. So it is important to be sure that the quest for ordinary greatness is reflected in the hiring process. Here are some ways to be sure that you are aligning your hiring process with spotting and creating ordinary greatness:

- Have a plan for recruiting ordinary greatness. What is your recruiting strategy? How do you find your best staff members? Are you purposeful, or do you simply place an ad in the newspaper and hope for the best? If you are having difficulty recruiting for ordinary greatness, here is a tip. Ask this question about every one of your staff members: "If I knew everything about this person that I know now, yet, pretending they did not work here, if they applied for their position, would I hire them?" If the answer is yes, you would definitely hire them again, find out how they were recruited or what mechanism, referral source, or relationship was tapped to get them on board. If you have five of these top staff members, you now have five proven strategies to recruit for greatness. If the answer is no, what are you doing about it? Are you coaching them, developing them, and letting them know where they stand? Even if you wouldn't hire them again, are you still looking for ordinary greatness in them every day?

- In the interviewing process, do not oversell the job or your company, hoping to get a quick agreement for hire in place. In his book, *Winning,* Jack Welch recommends that you "be sure you exaggerate the challenge of the open job; describe it on its worst day."[3] One Human Resources vice president of a hospital told us of a particular challenge with high turnover in the housekeeping department. The newly hired staff would often leave in the first week (sometimes even first day), and turnover in the department was quite high. When the vice president began to investigate and conduct exit interviews, she found that many of the staff were shocked they would have to clean up some disgusting messes, many of which were the result of patients' bodily functions. "No one told me I was going to have to clean up poop," one of them told the Human Resources vice president. She found out that the hiring manager was not being up front about the unpleasantness of the job for fear of scaring applicants away. But the path she chose was actually much worse. People were leaving the job after being screened and oriented at a huge expense to the hospital. Be positive during the process, but be open and realistic about the job. If you can scare them away by talking about some of the unpleasantness associated with the job, the applicant is probably not a good fit. Online shoe retailer Zappos.com takes this a step further. After one week of orientation, Zappos tries to bribe its employees to quit! Each employee is told, "Thank you for your time. If you leave the company now, we will pay you for your time, and we will also give you $1,000 to quit." The thinking is that if a new employee's commitment is so low that $1,000 could get them to leave, they are not a good fit. This practice started at Zappos with $100, then went to $500, is now $1,000, and the company is considering increasing the amount in the future. The price of not selecting ordinary greatness is high, and Zappos knows this.[4]

- Get others involved. When it comes to selection, do not trust your ability to select the right person alone. Avoid the lone genius trap. Have other members of the team interview the applicant. See if you can pull in some customers and vendors with whom the applicant might interact if hired. This decision is too critical to leave it to your gut. Another benefit to getting more people involved is gaining more engagement, buy-in, and friendliness toward the new employee.
- The job does not end with "You are hired." Pay attention to something human resources professionals call "onboarding." During the first few months of the employee's tenure, monitor the following:
  - Is the new staff person getting along with co-workers?

- Have mundane issues like business cards and computer access been taken care of?
- Is this person making friends or are they frequently seen eating alone?
- Are any of your veteran staff members responsible for helping the new person become familiar with the company and the culture?

The onboarding time frame is a tremendous opportunity to have conversations with the new staff member regarding behaviors. One of the most valuable pieces of feedback I (Brian) ever received was when I was still in my first few weeks with a company. After a meeting, I was pulled aside by a co-worker and told, "Brian, the way you acted in that meeting probably worked well for you the last place you worked, but here it will get you into trouble. That's not how we behave. You talked about yourself too much. Here, we give credit to the team."

Recognition

Entrepreneur Mary Kay Ash said, "There are only two things that people want more than sex and money . . . praise and recognition."[5] And so it is—everyone wants to feel valued. I (Pam) recently gave a speech on the importance of building a recognition culture at a mid-size organization in New Mexico. As I was packing my materials to leave, I noticed that a lady was standing in the back of the room nervously waiting. Finally she approached me and asked, "Can I talk with you?" As I looked up, I noticed there were tears in her eyes. "Of course you can," I replied. She went on to tell me that she recently celebrated 20 years of working for the company, and she had received a 20-year certificate. She was very proud of the certificate, but spoke quite emotionally about its delivery: Her supervisor walked by her desk one day and dropped a brown envelope containing the certificate on her desk without saying a word. She was devastated by this gesture and felt her many years of service to the company were unappreciated and for naught. Recognition is not about a piece of paper or a bonus or a gold pin. Recognition is about feeling valued.

Leaders get it—they understand how important recognition is in engaging the workforce—but they do not necessarily *do* it. Colleagues and authors of *The Transparency Edge: How Credibility Can Make or Break*

You in Business,[6] Barbara Pagano and Elizabeth Pagano, were intrigued with this divergence between thinking and behaving as it relates to recognition. Through interviews with leaders, the Paganos were able to identify the top nine reasons that leaders do not make employee recognition a priority. We have added our own commentary with each excuse.

9. *If I compliment people a lot, I might have a problem when performance appraisal time comes around—they will expect top ratings.* This excuse calls into question the importance of balanced feedback. If we let people know where they stand by providing a balance of both positive and constructive feedback, they will understand and there will be no surprises at performance appraisal time. In fact, performance appraisal day becomes the most anticlimactic day of the year, because performance discussions have been occurring every day.

8. *When people say they want reward and recognition, I think they mean more money.* Not so fast. Our experience is that people do not always expect a bonus or pay raise; they understand the financial realities of the business. But they know that it costs nothing to say a kind word, to thank them for their hard work, and to praise them when they get results and for their contributions to the team.

7. *I know it is important, but I forget.* Leaders need to put it at the top of their list—their employees do! Make a point every day of looking for opportunities to praise your staff. If you look for it, you will find it! We advise our clients to pass along some kind of positive praise to each employee at least every seven days.

6. *I do not need a pat on the back, and I think they really do not care about it either.* The assumption that others feel the same way as you do is a common mistake of leaders. Some leaders claim they do not need recognition; therefore, they aren't going to give any to their staff members. This unfair approach presumes that just because you may not want a lot of recognition, neither do others. We have yet to meet the leader who could not respond affirmatively to the question, "Has anyone ever positively praised or recognized you in a way that you remember years later?" See, you do like positive recognition! Now, start passing it along to your staff!

5. *They might get a big head and stop doing their work.* This is the big urban legend of leadership. Studies show that employees who

receive frequent recognition have higher self-esteem, are more confident, demonstrate more willingness to take on new challenges, and are eager to contribute their ideas to the betterment of the organization. We have never met an employee who found recognition and praise de-motivating. Mark Twain once said, "I can live for two months on a good compliment."

4. *If I compliment one, the others will think I am playing favorites.* So no one gets recognition? Remember, when turnover comes, your best people will leave first because they have the most options— everyone wants them. Playing to the lowest common denominator from a recognition standpoint could send your top performers running into the arms of a competitor who is better at spotting and celebrating ordinary greatness.

3. *I do not see any reason to recognize people.* Are you looking? Remember—positive praise at least once every seven days. That will not be accomplished staying in your office reading e-mail all day—get out and see and be seen. One of our favorite books is *Never Eat Alone*, by Keith Ferrazzi.[7] It is full of ideas on how to network, stay visible, and make a difference.

2. *Why should I compliment someone for doing good work? It is their job. That is what they are paid to do.* People are paid to do their job. Rewarding and recognizing people for good work is the job of leadership. If your people are doing their job, are you doing yours?

1. *I am too busy.* Employees know leaders are busy. It is exactly that knowledge that makes your recognition even more valuable. By recognizing them, you are giving them priority over something else. Nothing means more to people than knowing you gave of yourself to recognize them. If they thought you had nothing better to do, it would not mean as much.

Personal recognition has the greatest impact. A former colleague, Bette, has a dynamic personality that is reflected in her preference for recognition—she wants very public recognition with big celebrations. However, Karen, another former colleague, would be mortified should someone recognize her in a public venue. Karen is much more comfortable receiving recognition privately and in a very low-key manner. It may be the very same recognition to both colleagues, but its reception will be based on its delivery. Do you know the preferences of each of your employees? Do you match that preference with the delivery method?

Organizations are trying new strategies for recognizing the time and effort employees invest in doing their jobs well. Among them are plans for rewarding not just individual employees, but their families as well. With rewards ranging from simple handwritten letters of appreciation sent to the employee's home, to workplace luncheons and tours, to access to corporate transportation, and even personal chefs, organizations are discovering "the marriage of employee and family motivation" leads to greater employee engagement and retention.

Matthew Kelly, president of Floyd Consulting, relates this story:

> [We] were contacted by a janitorial company that had huge employee engagement problems. With 400 employees, the company's turnover rate was 400%. Initially, the company surveyed employees to find out why they were quitting and found many just didn't have transportation to work. The company set up a shuttle service in three different neighborhoods. By doing just that, turnover dropped to 225%.

> But there was still more work to be done. I said, "People don't dream of being janitors, so you have to find out what their dreams are and connect their work to their dreams." . . . The firm hired a full-time dream manager, who met with employees and their families once a month to identify their dreams and help them develop a plan to achieve them.

"When employees start engaging their families in their dreams, that's where you find the most passionate relationships," Kelly says, noting the company's turnover rate for its now-600 employees has dropped to 20%. "There's nothing more powerful than people pursuing their dream together."[8]

Perhaps the ultimate recognition is that given to an employee's loved ones. Having experienced this myself, I (Pam) can attest to its impact. When my daughter graduated from high school, she received a simple handwritten note from an executive colleague. The note read, "Jenna, congratulations on this great achievement. The world is waiting for you to make a difference. Your Mom mentions you often and with such pride. I enjoy working with your Mom and find she inspires me with her commitment to doing the best job possible." Speaking of handwritten notes, I (Pam) recently had the experience of a colleague who brought me a note I had written her 15 years before. She had kept it all these years. I had written the note to her when we served on a community board together before we became colleagues. You never know what the future will bring, the connections that will be made, or the impact that a simple note might have.

Employee Involvement and Participation

The latest generation of employees (sometimes called Generation Y) has been engaged in decision-making by their families and schools in ways vastly different than in previous generations. Children now have a significant say in most key family decisions, such as which house to purchase, which car to buy, and where the family will vacation. Generation Y is bringing this desire for involvement into the work-place, and leaders who feel they can continue to manage as they always have will be shocked when they not only fail to see greatness in their staff, but when they see management habits that worked in the past, such as maintaining secrets, playing politics, and promoting factions, cause their personal and professional demise. Our survival depends on engaging our staff and getting their best ideas.

> Imagine if 1 percent of the ideas, improvements, and solutions swimming in the minds of our workers were acknowledged, considered, and implemented. Our world would change in remarkable ways, and America would gain a huge economic advantage.[9]

When we are hired by organizations to help leadership teams get their staff more involved in the organization, to help them capture staff ideas and put those ideas to work, we often start by talking to people about why they are *not* submitting ideas or making suggestions. In nearly every case, the staff's response is that at one point a suggestion was offered, an idea was shared, or a better way was put forward, but it was treated with disrespect (in the perception of the employee) either by being ignored, cast aside, or never acted upon. The message continues to be: *Respect* us enough to follow through on our ideas, or at least tell us why you cannot.

After conducting these meetings, we challenge the leadership teams with the following questions: Do you respect your staff? Do you respect your customers? Do you respect others enough to treat them and their ideas with dignity and meaning? The knee-jerk reaction is "of course we do." But when we ask the leaders whether they respect others enough to genuinely listen to their ideas, capture them systematically, follow through on them, and when necessary, tell the people submitting the ideas why they cannot be put into practice, the leaders know they fall short of the respect standard. Respect is critical to relating to others, and like anything great, it is found in the smallest things.

Ryne Sandberg played second base for the Chicago Cubs for 15 seasons, and retired in 1997, recognized as one of the greatest second basemen to ever play the game. He made ten consecutive All-Star appearances and won nine consecutive Gold Gloves from 1983 to 1991. His career .989 fielding percentage is a major league record at second base. His story is remarkable because he was almost ignored by scouts. He was drafted in the 20th round of the 1978 amateur draft by the Philadelphia Phillies, who tried to make him a shortstop; the Phillies traded him to the Chicago Cubs after the team management determined Ryne would never be a big-league shortstop.[10]

They were right. Sandberg would never be a big-league shortstop. Shortstop is not where his greatness would be exposed. The Cubs placed him at second base, and he was arguably the best player ever to play that position. During his Hall of Fame induction speech, on July 31, 2005, Sandberg talked about how he played the game and showed respect to his teammates, his competition, and his game:

> The reason I am here, they tell me, is that I played the game a certain way, that I played the game the way it was supposed to be played. I don't know about that, but I do know this: I had too much respect for the game to play it any other way, and if there was a single reason I am here today, it is because of one word, respect. I love to play baseball. I'm a baseball player. I've always been a baseball player. I'm still a baseball player. That's who I am.

The fourth major league game I ever saw in person, I was in uniform. Yes, I was in awe. I was in awe every time I walked on to the field. That's respect. I was taught you never, ever disrespect your opponent or your teammates or your organization or your manager and never, ever your uniform. Make a great play, act like you've done it before, get a big hit, look for the third base coach and get ready to run the bases, hit a home run, put your head down, drop the bat, run around the bases, because the name on the front is a lot more important than the name on the back. That's respect.

My managers like Don Zimmer and Jim Frey, they always said I made things easy on them by showing up on time, never getting into trouble, being ready to play every day, leading by example, being unselfish. I made things easy on them? These things they talk about, playing every day, that was my job. I had too much respect for them and for the game to let them down. I was afraid to let them down. I didn't want to let them down or let the fans down or my teammates or my family or myself. I had too much respect for them to let them down.[11]

Respect. Do you respect those you lead enough to listen to their ideas and to involve them in decision making? Respect is often a feeling defined by our actions. People respected Sandberg because he respected them and the game. Give respect, and you will get it.

The words "I didn't want to let my team down" speak to the power of teams. Teams take an individual's commitment to another level and create a forum for engagement that cannot be achieved individually. Socialization is a basic need for the human spirit, and teams provide the opportunity to forge relationships while delivering organizational results. Teams provide the bond that staff need to feel part of something larger. Organizations also benefit from the collaborative efforts of many voices and perceptions of a team to get to the best idea or resolution. Patrick Lencioni says "The biggest opportunity for competitive advantage is sitting right under our noses—getting people to work together. There is simply no better tool for ensuring success and sustainability than building real teamwork at the top of the organization."[12]

Accountability

Accountability is nothing less than keeping promises. It is committing to a course of action and following through with those actions. Every organization understands the importance of systems and processes that promote accountability. This is very important, for without accountability, much of our time will be wasted on efforts that are not sustainable. But what about personal accountability? Are leaders held personally accountable in your organization?

For accountability to be truly effective, it must be visible in three ways. In a podcast on a different topic Dr. Joel Hunter[13] sparked these thoughts:

1. *Confrontational Accountability.* The French have a saying ("*On nes' appuie que sur ce qui résiste*") that translated, means: "We only lean on that which resists." For accountability to take root in your organization, leaders must be confronted when their behavior falls short of cultural norms. If we are to lean on one another, there must be resistance to our negative behaviors. This can take many forms: tough conversations, coaching for improvement, 360 feedback—these can all be effective methods of confrontational accountability. Too many organizations try to skip this part of accountability, as it can be unpleasant. This is a very powerful way to build the attribute of accountability into your organization's culture, and it is vital.

2. *Inspirational Accountability.* Have you ever worked for a leader for whom you performed simply because you did not want to let them down? These leaders inspire us, and this is a type of accountability. Great leaders confront, but they also inspire. Most inspirational accountability is done by example. Do your actions inspire accountability in others? Do people do the right thing because they know what you expect?

   Colonel Jerome Penner, at Fort Drum in New York, is such an inspirational leader. Colonel Penner leads the Medical Department Activity supporting the 10th Mountain Division, and every day at 1700 hours during the traditional Retreat ceremony, he inspires each of his soldiers to stop what they are doing and salute the flag when it is being lowered. One day he was being driven across base in the pouring rain by a young private who, without being told, pulled the vehicle to the side of the road at 1700 when he heard the firing of the cannon that signified Retreat, and he and the colonel stepped outside the vehicle and saluted as their clothes were soaked. A few minutes later, after the colors had been lowered signifying completion of the ceremony, they got back in the vehicle, and the private said, "I trust that was the right thing to do, even in the rain, Sir." Colonel Penner responded, "We always do the right thing, especially when nobody is watching." Colonel Penner says he was proud that his lesson had stuck. He had inspired the private to excellence. What a positive way to hold people accountable.[14]

3. *Motivational Accountability*. What motivates you? Is it taking care of your customers? Are you accountable to them? Yes, accountability can come from our customers. They need us, and they are why we get a paycheck. If we think more about their needs and what we must do to help them, it is a wonderful form of motivation, especially for those in the human services industry. But any industry can make a connection to serving others. This motivation may be the missing piece to your accountability puzzle. Do you share customer feedback with your staff? Do you promote motivational accountability? This type of accountability recognizes that we are needed by someone and that we are making a difference in someone's life.

To reach our highest potential, each of these types of accountability must be practiced by leadership and supported through systems and processes endorsed by the organization. Who needs you to be accountable today?

All three forms of accountability require a specific type of dialogue to be successful. "Driven discussions" are targeted exchanges focused on the progress and outcomes of agreed-upon measurements that drive job success. These are discussions that drive results. While it seems like these discussions would take place on a frequent basis between staff and managers, experience tells us this is not so. Instead, routine performance discussions are more likely to be a broad overview of the work being done without pushing to ensure that incremental progress toward the established goals is being made. Situations like the following are all too common:

Manager: Jayne, I am concerned with your performance. You are over three months behind in implementing the new raw materials inventory log.

Jayne: I am a little taken off-guard. I know I have been involved in the meetings to discuss the inventory log, but I did not realize I was responsible for implementing the system. We have never discussed that, and I have been concentrating most of my time around revising the financial reports.

Manager: Well, I assumed you understood your role, since I placed you on the committee. Now we are behind schedule, and unless we can do a quick catch-up, there is no way we will have the system in place for the new year.

The first step to avoid discussions like this one is to ensure that both the staff member and the manager are on the same page with respect to the goals, actions, steps, and time frames. It is best to document these commitments in writing for ease of reference in checking the process and progress and for reaffirming the focus and priorities.

Many performance management systems on the market provide a structured approach to managing goals and outcomes. We believe these systems can be quite beneficial. However, for maximum effectiveness, the performance system must be aligned with ongoing discussions between the manager and staff member. We recommend starting with the following questions:

Driven Discussion Questions
- What has gone well?
- Where are you having challenges with meeting the targets?
- Is there anything you have not accomplished that you feel you should have?
- What assistance can I provide to help you meet your goals?
- Have any new opportunities come up that we should consider?

We find the preceding four strategies to be most effective in advancing ordinary greatness. By selecting people with a propensity for ordinary greatness, acknowledging their contributions, involving them in all aspects of the organization, and ensuring a culture of accountability, you can lay the foundation necessary to achieve an exceptional level of passion and commitment. Ordinary greatness will become "just the way we do things around here" in your organization.

Engaged, motivated, and committed individuals are the essence of any high-performing organization.

- What do you consider the most important ordinary greatness characteristics to screen for when selecting a new colleague?
- How would your colleagues describe a work environment where they were fully engaged?
- What systems do you have in place that support a culture of accountability?

Chapter 8

Cultivating the Potential for Ordinary Greatness

Bell has played, literally, before crowned heads of Europe. Why the anxiety at Washington Metro?

"When you play for ticket-holders," Bell explains, "you're already validated. I have no sense that I need to be accepted. I'm already accepted. Here, there was this thought: What if they don't like me? What if they resent my presence . . . ?"

—Violinist Joshua Bell, as quoted in "Pearls
Before Breakfast," *The Washington Post*, April 7, 2007[1]

C ultivating the potential of the workforce is the greatest missed opportunity we see in today's business world. Quite simply, everything an organization needs to be incredibly successful already resides within that organization. Unfortunately, most organizations fail to see the greatness that already exists, missing opportunities to build on it for the greater good. Our earlier definition of ordinary greatness spoke to these unrecognized characteristics, qualities, skills, or efforts. Yet something was missing—we soon realized that a fuller definition of ordinary greatness must include a reference to the unrealized potential for greatness (see Exhibit 8.1).

Or•din•ar•y Great•ness
Superior and often unrecognized characteristics, qualities,
    skills, or effort found in someone who may be otherwise
    undistinguished; sometimes discovered in response to
    unexpected circumstances.
The unrealized potential of individuals and organizations to
    fully use the passion, commitment, and energy within
    them.

Exhibit 8.1   Expanding the definition of ordinary greatness

While it is true that organizations miss opportunities because they
fail to see the greatness before them, most organizations also fail to see
the potential of the individuals and teams within the work environment,
opting instead to add content experts to the staff or to hire consultants
to bring the knowledge forward.

When this happens, incredible potential is never captured, deny-
ing both the organization and the individual opportunities to take
advantage of what could be. Instead, we are faced with an overwhelming number of disengaged employees, an epidemic of "presenteeism"
(present in body but checked-out in energy, enthusiasm, and commitment), and individuals who are miserable in their jobs.

Is there a quick, easy resolution? No. But it would be a significant step forward if each leader had a ready answer for the following
challenge, "What will it take for my employees to say at the end of
each day, 'I reached my fullest potential'?" All too often, conversations
between supervisor and supervisee are superficial. They avoid discussing the real issues that drive employee engagement and job satisfaction.
There is little conversation enabling leaders to discover the aspirations
and hidden potential of their staff members. We recommend five strategies to help generate valuable feedback that leaders can use to create a
work environment that fully uses the skills and talents of its workforce:
identify the source of motivation, understand strengths and opportunities for development, conduct aspirational conversations, build a strong
team, and commit to talent greatness. While many of you may be using
these strategies individually, combining them to drive a focused plan
for your workplace will give you an undeniable advantage.

Identifying the Source of Motivation

What motivates each person? What will make that individual feel they have made a meaningful contribution?

One young man has managed to be open to his potential for greatness, and thus has achieved self-actualization at a very young age. Characterized as a "philanthropic prodigy," to date 12-year-old Mason Park has generated more than $44,000 for charity. He continues to raise money through various simple fundraising efforts: selling bracelets and lemonade, washing cars, collecting cans, and writing letters and making telephone calls to potential donors. He has donated his proceeds to the American Diabetes Association, the American Heart Association, the Leukemia & Lymphoma Society, and other worthy charities. Motivated by a genuine sense of altruism, he shares his message on personally designed business cards: "It's the greatest thing in the world knowing you're a part of someone else's success . . . and that's what it's all about. People helping people."[2]

Mason's is an extraordinary story, made famous by various members of the media. But there are countless untold accounts of self-fulfilled individuals who share the same internal source of motivation to make a positive difference in another's life. We just have to make a conscious effort to recognize it for what it is.

Source of Motivation Questions
- What are two elements of a job necessary for you to be motivated?
- What is the biggest de-motivator for you?
- Which of your job responsibilities brings you the greatest satisfaction?
- Are any of your job responsibilities mundane or unfulfilling?
- You left work thinking to yourself, "I made a difference today." What occurred to make you feel that way?

Understanding Strengths and Opportunities for Development

Successful leaders are obsessed with discovering personal strengths and opportunities for development. They know that personal mastery and greatness come from a deep understanding of self. They focus on maximizing the strengths of individuals and developing them in areas where they are not quite up to par. Once these "development opportunities" are understood, a leader has three choices regarding them:

1. *Get help and try to improve them.* In a sense, this approach attempts to move weaknesses to the strengths category. It can be done, but it can be daunting, and will only work with some weaknesses. For example, a leader can probably become a better listener with attention and coaching, but can a person become expert dealing with budgets if they have no interest in or proclivity with finance? That is debatable. The point is to be purposeful about which perceived weaknesses you choose to develop, not to try to change base parts of your personality.

2. *Partner with people who have the strengths you do not have.* The writing of this book is a great example of this principle—one of us is a raging extrovert whose mind happily moves from concept to concept without completion. The other of us is an introvert who guarantees that one concept is in place and deliverable before a new one is created. For one of us to try to become like the other would be disastrous—we would both be miserable. In fact, recognizing our individual strengths and weaknesses has made us respect each other for developing the strengths we do not have, and it has allowed us to build a great friendship based on mutual respect. What are your development opportunities? Once your list is complete, find people who have your weaknesses as strengths and ask whether you can learn from them.

3. *Avoid tasks that require competence in your area of weakness.* This is another choice—recognize you have weaknesses and avoid putting yourself in situations where they are emphasized. If budgets, facts, and figures frustrate you, do not volunteer to take ownership of your department's budget process. If long-term planning is not your thing, do not apply for a job doing strategy. If you are an introvert who prefers to work alone, don't work at the information desk, where you will have to interact with many new people every day. In fact, this might represent an opportunity to develop your staff. That task you dread might be the thing they have been waiting

to do. This quote is attributed to legendary basketball coach John Wooden: "The worst things you can do for the ones you love are the things they could and should do for themselves."[3]

Successful leaders so "lock in" to their pursuit of understanding their strengths and weaknesses that it often carries over to their staff. Recently I (Brian) was traveling in North Carolina, and stopped at a Dairy Queen. Evidently, the law in North Carolina requires restaurants to prominently post their score from the last health inspection conducted by the state. This particular Dairy Queen had scored quite well, and I saw a giant "99.5" certificate posted by the cash register where I was placing my order. I commented to the young lady who was helping me that the 99.5 out of a possible 100 was a great score and congratulated her. Her response told me all I needed to know about the leadership of that restaurant. "It's good," she said, "but it's not good enough!"

This pursuit of strengths and weaknesses is vital, because it gives staff an opportunity to tell their stories and allows others to spot opportunities for ordinary greatness. Our friend Rich certainly is an example of this phenomenon. Rich worked in Finance and was a good employee. He did all that was required of him, yet he felt his boss, Karen, was not fully using his abilities to the benefit of the department. Rich courageously asked for a meeting where he could "tell his story," share his strengths, and discuss how he might improve in the areas he considered himself weakest. Karen graciously agreed to meet. Toward the end of the meeting there were two lists: Rich's and Karen's. Each identified Rich's strengths and weakness; however, the lists were not identical. After further discussion, they agreed on the top strengths and the top areas for improvement. An "aha!" moment for Karen was recognizing Rich's organizational skills. She discovered that not only was he good at organization, he was consumed by it. He was a master at keeping projects with lots of moving parts running smoothly. Karen had heard of a need within the organization for someone to take ownership of logistics and planning for the quarterly leadership development sessions, involving hundreds of leaders. This responsibility would be in addition to his regular job in Finance, and Rich jumped at the chance. He planned every aspect of the day, from parking to registration to feeding two meals to more than 500 leaders, out-of-town guests, and guest speakers. His eye for logistics was amazing—and no one had ever noticed. Well, they noticed now, because every session that he planned was witnessed by all the leaders in the company. His example was not wasted. Today Rich is still with the company, and is responsible for all inventory tracking, supply purchasing, and warehousing. He is the beneficiary of candid discussions about his strengths and the areas that he needed to develop with a leader who knew how to create the opportunity for greatness.

Strengths and Opportunity for Development Questions:
- What do you consider your greatest strengths?
- What are the areas you feel are *not* your strengths?
- When your peers give you feedback about what they have observed about you, what do they say you do best?
- Likewise, what are two areas in which your colleagues might indicate that you could do better?
- If you were promoted tomorrow, what might your peers list as the reason(s) that you received the promotion?

Conducting Aspirational Conversations

Do you know the aspirations of each of your employees? Do you know where they want their careers to go in the next five years? Aspirational conversations are ongoing dialogue between the individual and their manager focused on personal development actions to support the expansion of responsibilities, upward mobility, or new career paths.

I (Pam) always like to end a team meeting by asking each person to share something personal about themselves. I find it breeds a tremendous sense of camaraderie. During one meeting, I asked each person to consider all the careers possible and choose the one they would most want for themselves. As we went around the room, each person shared their "ideal career" with commentary. Eventually, it was Jack's turn. Jack was the youngest and most inexperienced member of the team. He rarely commented in our meetings, spoke in a subdued voice, and was generally quiet and reserved in all his dealings. However, as his turn came, he quickly jumped up and said, "I want to be a motivational speaker. I want to influence people in a positive way." You could have heard a pin drop in the room. Then, someone offered encouragement, and another team member offered to share a set of tapes from an established motivational speaker. Jack was on his way. Over the next several years, I strategically placed Jack in situations where he would need to socialize and speak before groups. He struggled at first, given his introverted personality, but over time he became more comfortable. It was a great day when Jack proudly told me he had taken a position as head of an organization focused on improving the potential of disadvantaged youth. Jack had found a venue to realize his dream of motivating and inspiring others.

The leader open to spotting and developing ordinary greatness will see the value of conducting aspirational conversations with subordinates. We have been stunned by how few leaders actually do this simple, free activity that will reap benefits forever. Instead, experiences like this are more likely to be the norm:

A few years ago, we were working with a client, an urgent care center in the northwest United States. The leader was having issues engaging and retaining staff, as well as keeping patients happy. It did not take us long to figure out why. On our first tour of the center with the leader, a patient care tech (PCT) approached us, and said to the leader:

PCT: "Excuse me, boss, but I'm resigning my position. What paperwork do I need to complete? Is that something you can help me with, or do I need to go to HR?"

Leader: "You're leaving? What a surprise! What are you going to do?"

PCT: "I just got a job as a nurse at the hospital."

Leader: "Nurse? But you're a PCT!"

PCT: "Oh, I just graduated nursing school, and I am out of here!"

Evidently, the leader never knew the PCT was interested in becoming a nurse, or had enrolled in nursing school two years earlier, or had recently graduated. In short, this signified a lack of aspirational conversations, and our coaching with this leader focused immediately on this effort.

Do you know what motivates and inspires your staff? Do you know their aspirations? Do you talk to them frequently about this?

Here is a bit of a script with questions we have seen leaders use with success. WARNING: Do not read this verbatim to your staff. Instead, read our ideas to get an essence of what an aspirational conversation sounds like, and be yourself. Do not fake it or try to manipulate others using these questions and the subsequent information gleaned. This survey can be done in writing, but we recommend a human-to-human conversation. Some staff may need to be given a copy of the questions in advance to review them before the conversation.

"One of my goals this year is to facilitate a process that allows me to become more familiar with the remarkable talent here: you. I want to spend a few moments talking about any goals and aspirations you may have. My role in helping you develop is one I take seriously, and I appreciate your cooperation. I know that this conversation will reap great rewards for both of us."

Aspirational Questions
- What are two of your skill areas you would like to further develop?
- What is a new skill or talent you would like to pursue this year?
- If you had unlimited time and money to spend on your career development, how would you invest them?
- Is there a specific position at this company you would like to move into at some point?
- Where do you see your career going in the next three to five years?
- If I had a magic wand and could grant you success in any career of your choosing, what would you choose?
- What can I do to support the development of your career?

During the aspirational conversations, take notes, *listen*, and at the end of the meeting, assure the employee you are committed to continuing the dialogue and will follow up within two weeks to help them create a personal development plan based on the conversation. Investing in your employees on this level tells them you are interested not only in what they are doing for you, but also in what you can do to help them move forward personally and professionally.

After learning about what motivates employees, their strengths and opportunities, and their aspirations, you have a solid foundation for a plan to maximize each individual's potential for greatness.

Building a Strong Team

Another strategy for becoming the type of organization that attracts high-performing employees is a commitment to training and development. Continual learning is becoming an increasingly important option for high-performing job seekers. In fact, recent graduates surveyed listed happiness, career development, challenging work, training and development, and a good relationship with their manager as the most important aspects of a job. What makes them leave? The same survey states that poor promotional opportunities, unfriendly colleagues, poor starting salaries, uninteresting work tasks, and poor management style have them heading for the door.[4]

Employers around the world face the constant challenge of attracting and retaining the employees they need. According to global consulting firm Watson Wyatt, "Employers that are the best at building and maintaining the right work force are often the best at aligning workers' rewards with the company's goals. Their performance management programs clearly communicate what workers need to do to get ahead and to improve company performance. This builds a sense of teamwork that makes it easier to retain employees, as well as attract high-potential newcomers."[5]

Making a true commitment to developing the workforce is a significant endeavor that can be overwhelming at first. We recall a discussion with a CEO of a large resort with multiple locations throughout a sizeable metropolitan area. When we advised a systemwide development initiative as a leadership alignment strategy, the CEO's first comment was, "We have never brought all our leaders together in any kind of gathering." His second comment was, "There is no way we can afford to pull all our leaders off the job to attend a training session." Both comments spoke volumes.

It is almost impossible to align leadership across geographic locations and multiple facilities with different administrators unless there is consistency in messaging, expectations, and learning and development. The misalignment of leadership in this organization was one of the significant issues we identified early on in the consultation. When the CEO mentioned they could not afford to pull leaders off the job, he was speaking not of the financial impact, but concern that the organization could not function for a day without leaders watching over things. Our concern was a bit different—why could the organization not function without leadership watching over the shoulders of its employees? Obviously, an important attribute of high performance was missing from this organization.

Here is the rest of the story. The CEO finally gave in to our repeated recommendations, albeit reluctantly. The first all-leader session was such a resounding success that the organization now gathers all 700 of its leaders once each quarter for a day of learning. Now, when asked about the strategies that have propelled the organization to new levels of achievement, the CEO mentions its commitment to developing people. This is a great demonstration of walking the talk and delivering on the statement, "Our employees are our greatest asset."

A strong training and development initiative provides a substantial advantage in recruitment and retention of great employees. Other benefits include:

- An environment where top employees get excited and stay with the organization because they know there is a strategy for grooming, developing, retaining, and rewarding star performers. In return, they are willing to make a long-term commitment, work hard, and serve as advocates who promote the organization to potential co-workers.
- A system to coach underperformers or misfits to either an acceptable level of performance or out of the organization. By the way, one of the most common complaints we hear from employees is that underperformers are allowed to stay within the organization. Nothing depletes staff engagement more quickly than working beside colleagues who are obviously lacking skills, positive attitude, motivation, or the desire for success.
- A senior leadership team whose wisdom and experience is used in coaching and developing the next generation of leaders. The result is the preservation of institutional knowledge. The barriers, potholes, and challenges, as well as proven strategies for success, remain on the radar screen.
- Finally, perhaps the obvious: financial repercussions. When promotions come from within as a result of the training organization's training and development efforts, the cost of headhunters, search

firms, and recruitment advertising is avoided. Money and time are saved and put to much better use.

Committing to Talent Greatness

There is a common refrain, "We must get the right people with the right skills in the right place at the right time." No argument there. But unlike financial assets that are carefully monitored, human assets are often overlooked, unappreciated, and underdeveloped. Leaders in high-performing organizations think and act differently than their counterparts in under-performing organizations when it comes to their people. They lead rather than manage, are visible, adhere to a core set of behaviors, and are personally engaged in the success of their staff. The organization provides the structure for leaders to be successful in this endeavor through a well-planned talent management program that aligns efforts in attracting, engaging, and retaining employees.

Most companies respond positively to having a talent management program in place. But if you look deeper into the functionality and use of such approaches, you will most likely find disconnects that render it little more than a bureaucratic exercise. Research by McKinsey & Company indicates that few companies have made managing talent an integral part of their long-term strategy.[6]

We consistently find five reasons that typical talent management programs lack what is needed to drive ordinary greatness and organizational success:

1. The strategy is seldom used and only occasionally deployed to build talent. It has been developed and resides in the policy and procedure documentation, but has little or no relevance in day-to-day operations.

2. The program is not aligned with strategic business strategies and emerging business needs. A talent management strategy may exist, but it is a stand-alone element, not an integral part of the organization's vision and plan for the future. The development component of the strategy is not aligned with business needs, so leaders are not being prepared for the future, but are developed for the status quo, gaining skills and knowledge that will likely be irrelevant in the future.

3. Senior executives are not intimately involved. Building a commitment to talent management requires that senior executives have a passion for talent management, demonstrated through their support and participation in coaching, mentoring, and teaching.

4. Talent management is restricted to promoting leaders to higher levels of leadership, rather than focusing on the development of each individual within the organization. Talent management initiatives should provide opportunities for everyone in the organization to grow and develop, from the entry level positions to the executive suite. That is what ordinary greatness is about—it knows no bounds.

5. Developing talent is not part of every leader's role and responsibility. There is no clear expectation that developing the organization's talent is an essential component of every leader's job.

Instead of "talent management" with the above pitfalls, a "talent greatness" mindset will reap greater rewards for you and your organization. Talent greatness goes beyond the scope of the traditional talent management strategy of attracting, engaging, and retaining staff to uncovering the hidden talents of every individual, growing that talent, and aligning it with business strategies supported by the organization's culture. Talent greatness becomes the organization's personalized value proposition to attract new staff and retain existing staff. Here is why:

- Instead of seldom-used random guesswork, talent greatness is ingrained into the DNA of the organization, because every leader uses this approach every day with every staff member. In this way, talent greatness is a more realistic approach, because no one has to wait on senior leadership to get a program started.

- Talent greatness tactics can be perfectly aligned with the business strategies of the organization, because each leader can reference the business strategies during aspirational conversations and coaching. This type of agility and flexibility removes a tremendous impediment to coaching—formality and stiffness.

- Senior leadership is more likely to be engaged in talent greatness than a mere HR-driven talent management program, because it requires senior leaders to discuss their favorite topic: the business. The more involved senior leadership is in any endeavor, the greater its chances for success.

- Talent greatness is not merely restricted to "who are we going to promote?" or "who should take my place?" conversations. Instead, this talent greatness attitude is "every, every, every." It permeates *every* conversation, *every* coaching opportunity, and *every* decision made in the organization.
- The typical talent management program is hit-or-miss. Talent greatness is incorporated into the 90-day plan of every leader with accountability for action. Recognizing greatness, celebrating greatness, and promoting greatness become the leadership brand of the organization, as well as the way to lead and teach others to lead. A great mantra to keep in mind: "Your company's leaders teach your company's leaders how to be your company's leaders."

Father James Keller once said, "A candle loses nothing by lighting another candle."[7] At this point, you are so close to ordinary greatness, you would definitely be able to spot it in a crowded Metro station.

One of the greatest joys of leadership is helping others achieve what they never thought possible.

- Do you know the aspirations of those you lead?
- How are you encouraging the potential of those around you?
- What is the leadership legacy you hope to leave?

Chapter 9

Changing the Way You View the World

Gene, your writing normally doesn't make me cry, to say the least. This story did and it was also sent to me by a friend who described it as "heartbreaking." I cried because I find it scary and depressing to think of how obliviously most people go through daily life, even smart and otherwise attentive people. Who knows what beautiful things I've missed by just hurrying along lost in my thoughts? It's almost a panicky feeling, that if a performance by Joshua Bell on his Strad[ivarius] gets lost in the shuffle, what about all the smaller beautiful things that happen every day and could be making people happier, if only they paid attention?

—Blog post from Boston, MA on the article "Pearls Before Breakfast," *The Washington Post*, April 7, 2007[1]

We have talked about leadership behaviors that help identify, recognize, and maximize greatness, but success is achieved by those who change their deeply rooted views of the world around them. It is a personal challenge to think and behave differently. Only when an individual has achieved this status is he or she truly open to the greatness that exists right before them. Changing the way you view the world will open opportunities you have never seen before.

We are reminded of a passage from Richard Bach's book, *Jonathan Livingston Seagull*:

> Don't believe what your eyes are telling you.
>
> All they show is limitation.
>
> Look with your understanding,
>
> Find out what you already know,
>
> And you'll see the way to fly.[2]

While there may not be anything amazing, astounding, or new about our recommendation to reassess how you view the world, it does require a change of habit, and that is always difficult to accomplish. Remember this joke: "How many people does it take to change a light bulb?" Answer: "Four. One to change the bulb and three to reminisce about how good the old light bulb was." Change can be motivating, exciting, and move us to greatness.

Take a few minutes to challenge yourself by responding to the assessment that follows. Let it guide you in determining where you can "get outside your comfort zone" and open your eyes to the greatness already there for you to see and appreciate. Through greater recognition of the extraordinary deeds of others, as well as your own potential, you will find more joy, more happiness, and more fulfillment in your everyday life.

Is Every Moment of Your Day Scheduled?

In today's world, we tend to have a "check the box" kind of existence. Sadly, we have become a society of listmakers whose greatest joy is in checking things off item by item as they are completed. Nike's slogan is "Just Do It!" and comedian Larry the Cable Guy exhorts us to "Git 'er done." These are the mantras by which we seem to live our lives. In our determination to fulfill one obligation after another in our personal and professional lives, multitasking (doing many things at once) has become common. As a result, there is no time for exploration and very little energy to look beyond the present moment. Schedules, which rule our existence, keep us from slowing down enough to consider the ramifications of what is happening in our daily life, and they do not typically allow us the luxury of observing ordinary greatness in action all around us. Our schedule becomes the scale by which we measure productivity: "Look how many things I checked off my list today!" As a result, we don't determine our schedule; it determines us.

A whole new movement has actually arisen around the concept of slowing down, and there are activists devoted to fighting what they consider the abuse of time. One such individual, 73-year-old attorney Edgar S. Cahn, serves as the leader of the "slow movement." He created Timebanks USA, a nonprofit group that treats time as money in an effort to help people curtail overextended lifestyles. Members of the group exchange blocks of time called "time dollars." For example, one person may barter the minutes used to walk the family pet in exchange for the interval needed to buy groceries on the way home from work. While the bartering process is pragmatic in nature, Cahn's ultimate goal is shifting people's priorities—getting them to slow down long enough to value time and spend it on things other than adhering to a hectic schedule. "Time is the most precious thing we have," says Cahn. "Every hour we live, we never get it back."[3]

He encourages "random acts of slowness"—turning off the BlackBerry, having dinner with the family, taking a walk—in other words, slowing down the lifestyle.

The slow-down movement was catapulted into global consciousness with the publication of the book *In Praise of Slowness*, by London-based journalist Carl Honore. Characterizing himself as a former "speedaholic," he calls attention to the impact of frantic schedules on our health and overall well-being. His epiphany came one day when he was trying to figure out how he could shorten time spent with his son. Aghast, he realized that he should have been seeking a way to share more instead of less time with the boy. Honore partially blames technology for our seeming inability to "switch off" and function beyond the immediate moment; he promises that when we slow down, we will greatly enhance our ability to enjoy work, friends, food, and family.[4]

According to *Fortune* magazine, its new survey of senior Fortune 500 male executives offers surprising answers. Fully 84% say they would like job options that let them realize their professional aspirations while having more time for things outside work; 55% say they are willing to sacrifice income. Half say they wonder if the sacrifices they have made for their careers are worth it. In addition, 73% believe it is possible to restructure senior management jobs in ways that would both increase productivity and make more time available for life outside the office. And 87% believe that companies that enable such changes will have a competitive advantage in attracting talent.[5] The survey revealed that their overburdened schedules were robbing them of the very things that allowed them to flourish as human beings: spouses, children, friends, prayer, and sleep. They were losing the experience of life itself.

What is your schedule like today, tomorrow, and next week? Is there time on it to do the things critical to your ability to flourish as a human being? If not, how will you find the time to recognize ordinary greatness when it touches your day or that of someone close to you?

Would You Strike Up a Conversation with a Stranger?

What part of the United States you live in, your upbringing, and your personality all play a part in the likelihood of you talking to a stranger. For example, people who live in the southern United States are notorious for being more open, hospitable, and friendly than those who reside in the northern states. On the other hand, if your parents consistently said, "Never talk to strangers," this advice most likely became permanently lodged in your subconscious, influencing you as an adult. Finally, being an extrovert predisposes you to initiate dialogue with someone unknown, perhaps the person in line behind you at grocery store, sitting beside you on a plane, or patiently waiting for a customer service number to be called.

There is an enormous amount of literature written about how to break the ice and talk to people you do not know. The fact is, the majority of us are reluctant to initiate conversation with a stranger even when there is a specific reason for it. In this case, the blinder that we are wearing is the setting: a comfort zone we are reluctant to breach, one that is dictated by familiarity with or knowledge of the people in our immediate environment. As a result, we miss a lot of opportunities to learn, stretch our mental horizons, and discover that we are the strangers because of our inability to connect with others personally unknown to us.

In his book *Blue Highways*, author William Least Heat-Moon chronicles his travels across the United States taking the roads less traveled. He never met a stranger because of his open mindset; every setting was an opportunity to make a friend. As a result, he encountered numerous individuals whose lives were a testament to ordinary greatness. His storytelling of humble, down-to-earth people who did extraordinary things makes for fascinating reading.

There was the man in Shelbyville, Kentucky who was in the process of "rescuing" a piece of history—a 150-year old log cabin that had been built, in its time, with only hand tools, like an ax, adz, froe, and wedge. Heat-Moon watched as the man locked a crowbar onto a wooden peg, pulled it free, and handed it to him. The peg's color was much lighter than the logs, and amazingly, it smelled of freshly cut wood. "You're sniffing a tree from 1776 . . . Gives you a real sense of history," the man said. He told Heat-Moon that he was restoring the log home so that people "could be reminded," and in doing so, he felt he had "done something to last."

Then there was the story of Brother Patrick, a Trappist monk. A former ghetto cop in Bedford-Stuyvesant, he had tired of "the bleeding and the shot and the cut people" he was forever bandaging up—to say nothing of the 13 babies he delivered in police car backseats. So he left that line of work and eventually found his way to the Monastery of the Holy Spirit in the backwoods of Georgia. There he became known as Smokey the Monk, because he took on the job of overseeing the grounds. Just for fun, he catalogued all the wildflowers, identifying about 200 species before shifting focus to other flora. He told Heat-Moon that "simplicity reveals the universals we all live under. Here the effort is to free yourself from blindness, arrogance, selfishness . . . Coming here is following a call to be quiet. When I go quiet, I stop hearing myself and start hearing the world outside me. Then I hear something very great." Brother Patrick had succeeded in removing his own set of personal blinders, and in doing so left himself open to experiencing greatness.[6]

Do You Try New Things?

We are all creatures of habit and routine. Reflexively we cling to the familiar, the safe, the things that have worked for us in the past.

However, scientists tell us that unless we put forth an effort to learn, challenging the brain to create new neural pathways, it begins to atrophy. Think of the brain as a muscle: The more it is used, the stronger it becomes. One of the best ways to learn is to be open to new experiences.

The dominant characteristic of those who are continuous learners is curiosity. They want to know what it is like to play a musical instrument, cook a gourmet meal, create a quilt, or speak a new language. They are curious about people, places, and new skills. Gaining new knowledge and perspective becomes an end in itself.

One example of a historical person famous for his curiosity and the paths it led him down was Benjamin Franklin. Franklin's mind was never at rest; if one question was not plaguing him, another was, and he was always determined to satisfy his curiosity. He keenly understood that trying new things was a form of continuous learning; and putting that knowledge to use opened the door to more discoveries and valuable insight about situations and people.

As Postmaster General, Franklin pioneered the mail-order catalogue. He also invented a simple odometer for tracking the distance in mail delivery routes. He established the Union Fire Company with 30 volunteers, a prototype for the business of firefighting. His donation of 116 books to a town, ranging from *A Pilgrim's Progress* to treatises on religion and history, became the seeds for one of the first public libraries in the nation. His kite-flying experience led to the invention of the lightning rod as protection for ships and buildings. He created the Franklin stove, an iron furnace that could be placed in the center of the room, thus heating colonial homes more safely and efficiently. His poor vision resulted in the invention of the bifocal. The list goes on and on.[7]

Like Franklin, those who are curious are generally more engaged in life itself, always seeking stimulating activities and searching for novel experiences. They are motivated to find new ways of looking at the world, and find that when they do, the value of what they already know is enhanced. Well-known management expert Peter Drucker once said, "To make knowledge productive, we will have to learn to see both forest and tree. We will have to learn to connect."[8] The connection comes when a new experience results in transferring that newly acquired knowledge to the challenges, situations, and opportunities in other parts of our life. Benjamin Franklin was a master at this.

The bottom line: Being willing to try new things will help reveal what we previously failed to grasp. It helps us overcome numerous blinders that keep us from experiencing life to the fullest. It is just one more way of opening the door to possibilities, of being less closed off and more able to recognize ordinary greatness in the people with whom we interact.

Do You Learn a New Skill or Talent Each Year?

As children, we were unaware of our limitations, as any grade school teacher who gives out an assignment to write about "What I Want To Be When I Grow Up" well knows. At that point in time, the possibilities are endless.

But what happens? Eventually we learn to limit ourselves by our own perception of what we can or cannot do—or someone else applies that limiting label to us and it becomes self-perpetuating.

We recently had an opportunity to meet a gentleman who exemplified will, determination, and an attitude of unlimited possibilities. He will forever remind us of the ability we each have to learn under even the most extraordinary circumstances. In 1994, as a member of the U.S. Army Golden Knights skydiving team, Dana Bowman was performing in a routine training exercise high above Yuma, Arizona. Hurtling toward Earth with a partner, traveling at a speed of 300 miles per hour, the two collided in mid-air. Both of Dana's legs were severed instantly, and his skydiving partner was killed. Remarkably, Dana's parachute opened and he landed unconscious in a parking lot below, his life forever changed.

With extraordinary determination he dove into a punishing program of rehabilitation. Just nine months later, he returned to the Army by skydiving on prosthetic legs into his own re-enlistment ceremony—the first amputee member of the Golden Knights.

But his story does not end there. In 2000, he became the first member of his family to earn a college degree and graduated with honors, earning his bachelors' degree in commercial aviation. Today, he water-skis, snow-skis, scuba-dives, bicycles and leads a full, active life as a motivational speaker.[9]

The next time you are tempted to say something like . . .

- I wish I could speak Spanish—but I have no aptitude for languages.
- I could not possibly learn to play the piano; that is for kids.
- I cannot get an advanced degree; I am not smart enough.

. . . think of Dana Bowman, for whom accepting limitations was not an option.

Each of us has incredible potential, but the willingness to learn a new skill or acquire a new talent requires that we be determined to expand our horizons. In doing so, we will find that we think about the world in an entirely different way. Anything is possible, and we become more receptive to ordinary greatness. We find the blinder of preconceived notions melting away.

Do You Read at Least Six Books a Year?

Much research has been done about the benefit of reading when it comes to maintaining mental acuity. In fact, some studies suggest that people who do not perform the activities known to keep the brain sharp actually regress with respect to brain functioning. We have learned that people generate new brain cells and new connections between them throughout life. Mental stimulation is one key. The more you challenge your brain, the more new nerve pathways you form. It really is a matter of "use it or lose it."

Alarmingly, a study by a custom book publishing firm, the Jenkins Group, found that:

- One-third of high school graduates never read another book for the rest of their lives.
- 42% of college graduates never read another book after college.
- 80% of U.S. families did not buy or read a book last year.
- 70% of U.S. adults have not been in a bookstore in the past five years.
- 57% of new books are not read to completion.[10]

There is considerable research that explains why we do not read books any more—mainly, it is due to the copious accessibility of information via the Internet. However, the last statistic above—not reading books to completion—is another matter. It seems that it cannot entirely be attributed to a pinched availability of time. Rather, scholars suggest that we are in the midst of a sea change in the way we read and think, due to the Internet. Our very cognitive abilities are being rewired.

As part of a five-year research program, scholars from University College of London found that people who get their knowledge from online sources do it in a very distinctive way: They bounce from one source to another, rarely reading the piece in its entirety. The study reports: "It is clear that users are not 'reading' online in the traditional sense; indeed, there are signs that new forms of 'reading' are emerging as users 'power browse' horizontally through titles, content pages and abstracts going for quick wins. It almost seems that they go online to avoid reading in the traditional sense."

It is a different kind of reading, says Maryanne Wolf, a developmental psychologist at Tufts University. "The style of reading promoted by the Net, a style that puts 'efficiency' and 'immediacy' above all else, may be weakening our capacity for the kind of deep reading that emerged when an earlier technology, the printing press, made long and complex works of prose commonplace. When we read online, we tend to become 'mere decoders of information.' Our ability to interpret text, to make the rich mental connections that form when we read deeply and without distraction, remains largely disengaged."[11]

Reading helps us visualize the world as it truly is and remove the blinders of personal bias. It helps keep faulty information at bay so that we perceive things without slanted perceptions. It enlarges our immediate world and makes it far more possible to recognize the great deeds that ordinary people are doing all around us, every day. The verdict is still out on how the Internet will shape our capacity to read; we have to be aware of its potential to deflect us from the ability to think deeply and recognize ordinary greatness around us.

Do You Surround Yourself with People Who Think Differently than You?

If you are in the world of business, you already know the value of diversity. Work outcomes are greatly enhanced by team diversity because of the variety of perspectives, problem-solving methods, and ideas exchanged. It becomes much easier to have eyes "wide open" to potential and to recognize the extraordinary things that co-workers do professionally and personally. However, it is a different matter if the work environment is peopled with those who think alike and who prefer the safe and secure way of doing things.

Consider, for example, the concept of *groupthink*. It is defined as a psychological disorder that can seriously influence the decision-making process of a unified group. The individuals in the unit become less inclined to think critically, and the main priority of the group is their overall consensus. This sense of accord becomes so important that they go out of their way to protect it, fearing that the group will actually split up if they lose consensus. With their priorities changed, the group members become occupied with the group's goals and soon begin to think alike without question. Thus, groupthink is very much a downward spiral, with individuals becoming less distinct with time while developing the groupthink disorder.

The subject of groupthink has been studied extensively, but the most authoritative documentation on the subject can be found in the works of the concept's founder, Irving Janus. He wondered why intelligent groups of people sometimes made decisions that were not sound and that led to disastrous results. Focusing on the political arena, he studied controversial conflicts, such as the Bay of Pigs, the Korean War, Pearl Harbor, the Vietnam War, and the Cuban Missile Crisis. He believed the people responsible for decision-making in those situations were so engrossed with arriving at a consensus that they were unable to consider alternative, creative courses of action. This condition, which he named groupthink, can actually be considered another form of bias. People are so consumed with their interrelatedness that they refuse to consider what "outsiders" have to say or to embrace different ways of thinking.[12]

The flip side of this coin can be found in such innovative companies as Apple, Google, 3M, Toyota, and Microsoft. The "holy grail" for these organizations is a work environment peopled by individuals whose thinking is totally nonhomogenous, who can focus on all possibilities.

David Kelley, founder of the design firm Ideo, discovered his life-long mission through a most unusual route: being diagnosed with cancer.

"I was put on the planet to help people have creative confidence . . . to teach as many people as I can to use both sides of their brain, so that for every problem, every decision in their lives they consider creative as well as analytical solutions." Kelley is convinced cancer has given him more resolve to do this.

John Maeda, president of the Rhode Island School of Design, describes his friend Kelley this way: "The kind of person you aspire to become . . . an anonymous superstar."

David Kelley's determination to move from being a designer to a design thinker revolutionized every aspect of his life, personal and professional. Instead of focusing on the end result—a solution to a design challenge—he focused on the method or approach to the solution. Amazingly, when the approach was correct, the results consistently exceeded expectations.[13]

Bringing those who are different from ourselves into our lives can just as easily be achieved through a social dimension. Being involved with diverse volunteer groups whose mission is philanthropic in nature, community oriented, or faith based will help make us inclined to recognize people who perform deeds of ordinary greatness. Those who volunteer to serve others generally have a more highly developed sense of what blinders are: roadblocks to selfless acts that benefit others.

Are Your Best Friends a Carbon Copy of You?

While it is natural for your cadre of friends to have similar interests or backgrounds, this can be self-limiting. Those who are not carbon copies can be stimulating and enlightening. We can learn things from them that we would never be exposed to otherwise. Plus, their very dissimilarity prompts us to think about what else we might have been missing.

Author Jenny Uglow's book *The Lunar Men* is the story of a remarkable group of friends in mid-eighteenth-century England. She shares the history of the Lunar Society of Birmingham, who assembled in each other's houses on the Monday nearest to the full moon (so that they could see their way back home in the early hours). This fascinating, richly textured group of friends actually jump-started the Industrial Revolution! Among them were manufacturer Matthew Boulton; physician, poet, and biological theorist Erasmus Darwin; inventor James Watt; potter Josiah Wedgwood; and preacher and chemist Joseph Priestly.

They would get together in the early afternoon to eat, piling the table high with wine and "fish and capons, Cheddar and Stilton, pies and syllabubs." Their children played underfoot. Their wives chatted in another room as the Lunar Men talked well into the night, clearing the table to make room for their models and plans and instruments. Between meetings, they wrote to one another, cheering on the various projects each was involved with. Blending science, art, and commerce, this group of friends built canals; launched balloons; named plants, gases, and minerals; and changed the very face of England (along with the china in its parlors).[14]

This fascinating true story leads us to wonder how civilization might have developed without this group of men, as different as they were, becoming friends in support of each other. Each person's individuality spurred innovation on the part of others in the group, opened new creative doors, and fostered disparate ways of thinking. Were you and I to be fortunate enough to have friends so unlike us in our talents and way of living, we might be more inclined to see and be privy to ordinary greatness. The understanding of the power of diversity would tear down blinders such as compartmentalizing people and focusing only on their external attributes.

Are You a Risk Taker?

It is very obvious when a person is doing something that he or she was called to do. What may not be apparent is the risks those individuals took in order to fulfill their role in life. Earl Nightingale tells the story of a farmer who, as he trudged through a field, came upon a one-gallon glass jug tossed into his field. Nearby was a small pumpkin growing on a vine; he placed it in the jug without damaging the vine. The tiny pumpkin continued to grow—but only to a certain point. Once it filled the jar, it could expand no further. Its growth was essentially finished.[15]

The pumpkin can be likened to a number of people who limit themselves, who grow to a certain point and stop. Their enclosure is not a glass receptacle, but rather the refusal to take a risk. Inhibited by fear, complacency, or a lack of curiosity, they are also victims of various self-imposed blinders. Studies of children have revealed their innate ability to take a risk and never look back. A child likes trying new things, will take a chance just to learn of the outcome, and is not afraid of failure. Unfortunately, this openness is too often lost to most—not all—of us as we mature.

Research about elite athletes who participate in extreme sports has revealed their reasons for doing so: It is not so much about the achievement, but rather what one becomes through the process. They gain immeasurable self-confidence and liberation from constraints. Something is born inside them. Perhaps children know this instinctively and accept risk-taking as a natural part of growth.

There are countless stories of ordinary people who rise to the occasion and selflessly take risks that touch others' lives—consider occupations that are dependent on these individuals, such as firefighting, law enforcement, and lifeguarding.

Besides the aspect of heroism associated with taking risks, there are stories of those who unselfishly gamble when a human being's need is identified, and as a result achieve ordinary greatness. One such story is that of Oral Lee Brown.

Brown was waiting for a light to change so that she could cross an East Oakland, California street, back in 1987. She heard a voice asking her for a quarter, and she looked down to see a small child. Assuming the little girl wanted money for candy, she invited the youngster to accompany her to a nearby corner store. Instead of sweets, the child asked for bread and bologna to feed her family. Taken aback, Brown purchased the food, then asked, "Where's your mother? Do you go to school?" The little girl shyly replied, "Some time," and then ran off across the street.

Later, Brown found she could not get the incident out of her mind. Why was the girl out of school? What were the circumstances that had reduced her to begging? After several weeks of troubled sleep, Brown went looking for the child. She started at the local elementary school, where she visited a first grade classroom considered one of the worst in the area. Nearly all the children came from poor families who lived in violence-plagued neighborhoods. Few had two parents living in the household.

Brown did not locate the young girl that day. But she returned to ask the teacher if she could adopt that class, and then she took an enormous personal risk: on the spot, she promised all those kids a college education if they finished high school!

At the time, as a real estate agent, Oral Lee Brown was taking home just $45,000 annually.

Yet, years later she made good on her pledge. After 19 of the 23 students graduated, she sent them off to college. What was going on during the time the children were growing up? Brown became a surrogate parent, staying in close touch with them, encouraging, mentoring, and even tutoring them. After all, she had given them a vision for the future, a reason not to join the ranks of the three out of four students who dropped out of the local high school.

Her risk, as you can imagine, took an enormous toll on her life, turning it upside down. To prepare for the colossal tuition bill, Brown put $10,000 of her own money into a trust account each year. It was not easy, and she often worked multiple jobs, finally establishing a foundation that local businesses helped fund. In a 2005 interview, Brown said that right after she met with the children and their parents to explain what she intended to do, she sat in her car literally shaking. The enormity of the risky promise she had just given to 23 underprivileged youngsters was daunting. How would she make good on it?

But she had faith in her ability and believed it could be accomplished. Today, 18 of Brown's first-graders have graduated from college and 3 have gone on to graduate school. Hers is a story of compassion and hope; it is profound story of ordinary greatness based on taking a huge risk that few of us would even consider.[16]

Do You Look for the Lesson in Each Experience?

"Experience is the teacher in all things." The great Roman leader Julius Caesar recorded the earliest known version of this proverb in *De Bello Civili* (c. 52 B.C.).[17] Over the centuries, have we adhered to the words of this famous leader? History reveals that too often in life, the lessons we should be learning through experience are curtailed by the blinders we wear.

Learning authority David Kolb says that for the learning process to be effective, four behaviors must happen sequentially. First, we perceive the information; next, we reflect on how it will affect an aspect of our life. Third, we compare how it fits in with our own experience; and fourth, we reflect on how this information offers us new ways to act.[18] Steps three and four (comparison and reflection) can be greatly affected by personal bias and by being too busy to take the necessary time for reflection.

In addition, compartmentalizing also contributes to lessons not learned. We tend to pick and choose the individuals we deem capable of having experiences we can learn from. A prime example of this is gaining knowledge from how children experience life.

Dr. Fred Epstein was a world-renowned neurosurgeon who pioneered lifesaving procedures for children with insidious brain tumors. He established the division of pediatric neurosurgery at New York University Medical Center, and served as the founding director of the Institute for Neurology and Neurosurgery (INN) at Beth Israel Medical Center Hospital.

He also authored the heartwrenching book *If I Get to Five: What Children Can Teach Us About Courage and Character.* The title is based on the goals that one of Dr. Epstein's patients, a four-year-old girl named Naomi, set for herself as she battled a brain tumor. If she could just get through all the surgeries and the pain—if she could just get to age five—she knew she could learn to ride a bike, jump rope backward, and tie her shoes in a double-knot.

In this book, Dr. Epstein chronicles his journey into the hearts, minds, and souls of his wise young patients and the amazing lessons he learned from them. He admitted that surgeons in general tend to compartmentalize their professional and emotional lives, saying they are trained to believe the proper role is to remain objective professionals. Yet his young patients—whom he called his greatest teachers—taught him otherwise. In fact, he and his colleagues arrived at a paradoxical conclusion: the closer they got to their patients, the more strength and inspiration they were able to draw from them. By keeping their hearts, as well as their minds, open to the children, they learned professional and personal lessons that had eluded them earlier in their careers.

In Epstein's words, "I used to think that courage meant taking on the toughest cases, being the guy who dared to make the life-and-death judgment calls in the operating room. I now know that holding a child's hand while he undergoes chemotherapy can be a lot scarier than holding his life in my hands during an operation."[19]

This amazing and brilliant man had closed himself off all his professional life to the ordinary greatness of his young patients. Only when he allowed himself to be open to what they were experiencing did he learn a valuable lesson—compartmentalizing was the blinder that had kept him from seeing the obvious.

Do You Take Your Passions with You Everywhere You Go?

Mike Rowe, host of the television program *Dirty Jobs*, was asked by *Fast Company* magazine to share some tips and life lessons learned while traveling around the country spending time with people who do some of what most of us would refer to as disgusting jobs. Number one on his list was: "Never follow your passion, but by all means bring it with you." This struck us as great advice. Some say, "Follow your passion." Dumb advice. If I (Brian) simply followed my passion, I am afraid most days I would just toss the football around the backyard with my sons. I am most passionate about spending time with my family, but of course, that has to be balanced with a need to make money, fulfill other obligations, and so forth. So we love Mike's advice—take your passion with you wherever you go.[20]

Our background in organization development (OD) consulting has allowed us to do a lot of work with clients on capturing the "discretionary effort" of the workforce. What causes some employees to give more than is required, while others do the minimum? What causes some to stay late to get the job done, while others cannot wait to clock out? This seems to be the central question facing employers today. How do we get the maximum discretionary effort from every employee?

In most businesses, the greatest expense is not supplies or equipment; it is people, in the form of salaries and benefits. When we begin consulting with a new organization that is not doing well financially, it is often a safe bet that the biggest waste in the company is not in the supply room or warehouse. It occurs every time an employee goes home, thinking "I could have done more." "I could have given more."

"I could have been nicer to that customer, but who would have noticed?" "I could have followed through with my co-worker on a commitment I made, but who would have noticed?" Simple math proves this to be the case, since in most companies, those who go above and beyond the minimum are not earning substantially more than those who give the nondiscretionary, required effort just to keep their jobs. This fact alone is a source of huge frustration to the employees who give discretionary effort every day. They usually are not financially rewarded for it, so why do it?

Perhaps a big part of the answer is in Mike Rowe's advice. Some people have not brought their passion with them. Have you? Not "are you passionate about your work?" but "do you take your passion with you as you start all new tasks?"

Watching Mike's show gives some insight to this concept. While everyone he visits is doing a dirty job—and for the most part, it seems—not getting rich doing it, every person he works with is engaged and showing passion for their work. Can someone really be passionate about collecting chicken manure or scrubbing the inside of cement mixers? I doubt it. Instead, I think these people have brought their passion with them, and no matter what they do, they are passionate about it. Does it help to do work we find interesting? Of course. But we have also met executives who work in much nicer surroundings and make more money but who are miserable and exhibit far less passion for their work than do Mike's friends. They have a great job, but they have not brought their passion into that job with them.

If your workforce is made up of people who give the minimum effort required to keep their jobs but nothing more, you will never be a great company. How can we ensure each person is contributing their discretionary effort? Here are some ways to make sure people are bringing their passion with them to work:

- *Let them know you expect it.* Not in a manipulative "work harder," or "this year, let's do more with less" sense (both of those approaches are negative and will backfire); instead, in a clear way, let people know that part of the privilege of being on this team is that we will do more than is required. A company focused on providing extraordinary customer service will tap into everyone's discretionary effort by incorporating an inspiring call to action: "No one will outserve us!"

- *Hire for it.* Discretionary effort cannot be taught in a classroom. You have to find people who will bring it with them to work every day. Is your hiring model designed to find people who will perform more than the minimum and weed out those who have an entitlement mindset of "If I do more for you, boss, then I expect you to give me more"? One way to increase the odds of attracting those who live and work this way is to ask in the interview with a prospective employee, "Tell me about a time in your last job where you did more than your boss expected." If the prospective employee has no answer or no stories of how they have ever done this for anyone else they have worked for, what makes you think they will do it for you?

- *Recognize it.* When you see staff performing more than expected, recognize it. Let people know that in your company and in your department, the heroes are the ones that do more and give more. Every day, look for examples of staff members who serve more than is required, take more time with customers than is needed, and serve as an example to their fellow staff members in this area. In these times of staff cutbacks and resource shifting, you cannot afford to miss a recognition opportunity any time a person does more than is expected. Remember, this area reflects the greatest waste elimination opportunity in your company. This year's goal for you: *every staff member bringing his or her passion every day in every interaction!*

- *Role-model it.* Does staff see you giving more than is required? What do they see when they witness you interacting with customers? Do they see passion in you? Do you bring your passion with you every day? Do not expect those you lead to exhibit something they do not see in you.

Taking your passion with you everywhere you go is an important component of being able to spot ordinary greatness. Leaders who do this will be more open, more joyful, and able to spot greatness because misery will never get in the way. The commuters in the Metro station may have been passionate about some things, but most were not passionate *in that moment*. They did not take their passion with them on their way to work that day.

It was reported that President John F. Kennedy was touring the NASA Space Center in the early days of space exploration, and during the tour he met a custodian. President Kennedy asked, "What's your job around here?" The reply: "I'm putting a man on the moon!"

Growing up in West Virginia, I (Brian) heard the story of a country doctor who late one night was called out to the backwoods home of one of his patients, an expectant mother who was in labor. There was no electricity in the home, and the only light came from a lantern that the doctor asked the soon-to-be father to hold in the air close to him so the doctor could see what he was doing. After a few minutes, crying was heard, and sure enough, a new baby had arrived. The father, eager to see his child for the first time, put down his light, causing the doctor to cry out, "Lift that light again—there's another baby coming!" Sure enough, twins! So, again, the father placed the lantern on the floor, and the doctor exclaimed, "Where's that light? We have triplets!"

Amazed, the father asked, "Do you think the light is attracting them?"

Light attracts. Are you giving off light so that others may see ordinary greatness in you, and through you, see it in others?

The author of Ecclesiastes wrote, "Whatever your hand finds to do, do with all your might."[21] Take your passion with you, and you will spot ordinary greatness. And along the way, you will have more fun!

How Did You Do?

What did you learn about yourself from taking this assessment? Perhaps you discovered that you are closed off to experiencing life to its fullest. Perhaps you walk by opportunities for recognizing ordinary greatness because you do not force yourself to see things differently.

Perhaps this personal inventory has served its purpose: to demonstrate that we can learn to recognize greatness in the most ordinary of settings if we make a conscious choice to change the way we view the world.

Opening our eyes to ordinary greatness requires that we think and behave differently.

- What is the most significant area of opportunity for personal change in your life?
- What is one thing you can begin doing today that will make a difference in your ability to recognize and appreciate ordinary greatness?
- How do you carry your passion with you every day? Is it obvious to others?

Chapter 10

Ordinary Greatness in Challenging Times

Souza nods sourly toward a spot near the top of the escalator. "Couple of years ago, a homeless guy died right there. He just lay down there and died. The police came, an ambulance came, and no one even stopped to see or slowed down to look.

"People walk up the escalator, they look straight ahead. Mind your own business, eyes forward. Everyone is stressed. Do you know what I mean?"

—EDNA SOUZA, SHOE SHINER AT L'ENFANT
PLAZA, AS QUOTED IN "PEARLS BEFORE
BREAKFAST," *THE WASHINGTON POST*, APRIL 7, 2007[1]

As we were completing the manuscript for this book, the world's financial structure began a spiral of unexpected turmoil. Its impact continues to be felt far and wide. Today's economic environment is having a profound effect around the world, and its ramifications are becoming more and more manifest in the workplace. Our colleagues are nervous, afraid, and stressed, with concerns about personal situations adding to the everyday pressure of work. It is becoming overwhelming for some, if not most. Statistics indicate increased absenteeism, less focus on the job at hand, more conflict among co-workers, and a general feeling of apathy.

Almost immediately we began to get calls and e-mails from leaders across the globe asking the question, "How do I lead in such unprecedented and uncertain times?" "How do we focus on ordinary greatness when we are re-evaluating and redefining everything we know as 'normal'?" Excellent questions. It is more important than ever that leaders step up to the plate and lead in these turbulent times. Given this important call to action for leadership, we added this final chapter as the book was going to press.

We will rejoin John, the fictitious CEO we met in Chapter 4. One year later, we find John and his leadership team dealing with declining sales in all divisions over the past six months, due in large part to the recent economic downturn. Combined with a reduction in interest income, several low-cost suppliers have filed bankruptcy, requiring the company to purchase higher-priced raw materials and reducing the product margins to dangerously low levels. This has forced a series of meetings to determine strategies to deal with the challenges faced by the company.

Avoid Short-Sighted Decisions

John started the weekly meeting on a somber note. "Over the past several weeks we have had good dialogue regarding the impact of the current economic climate on our financial position. I appreciate everyone's contributions and focus on preparing the forecast. The latest numbers are in, and they are not pretty. It's clear that we must act swiftly to reposition ourselves to deal with what's ahead."

"Are you talking about significant cost reductions?" asked Rita.

"I don't think there is another way around it, but I would love to hear any ideas on how we are going to make up a $10 million shortfall over the next ten months," replied John. "But before we go there, let's talk about a process for coming to some conclusions about the actions that need to be taken."

"We just need to spend a day behind closed doors and make the tough decisions to get the ball rolling," suggested Chip.

"I think we need to set an across-the-board reduction percentage target for all managers and just get it done," stated Bill. "We did it that way back in 1986."

"I'm not sure I'm comfortable with that, Bill," replied Rita. "I remember that time too, and I also remember that we found later we'd cut some very valuable services and lost loyal customers because of it. We also lost some of our most talented colleagues. I don't think an across-the-board cut is the way to go. We need to be more strategic."

"Rita, we have to move quickly," replied Chip. "Taking an across-the-board cut will get us where we need to be, and we can't afford to wait. And it means we need to cut positions. What if we mandate a 5% reduction in salaries and wages in each department?"

In times of stress and financial uncertainty, leaders are often quick to make decisions that will have an immediate impact on the bottom line without careful consideration of the long-term consequences of those decisions. It is imperative that organizations identify critical areas that need to be preserved, including those that would likely affect customer satisfaction and product/service quality. Across-the-board reductions are a common response to a financial turnaround, but seldom position the organization for success. One of the best ways to avoid shortsighted decisions is to be inclusive while evaluating the pros and cons of various decisions. Remember, the view from the executive suite does not necessarily provide a panoramic picture of the day-to-day realities of company operations at the department level. Surely, unintended consequences will occur. Engaging leaders and front-line staff in the process of identifying areas to preserve as well as areas that can be reduced or eliminated will create greater support and mobilize employees to make and support the changes necessary to be successful in the new economic reality. Writer Tim Sanders states, "Agenda item number one is to tell people why they're great. People can doubt themselves in such troubled times."[2]

Increase Communications

"John, I'm sure I'm not the only one that has felt the escalating stress and anxiety among our workforce," said Carl. "Understandably, everyone is a bit tense about the impact on their personal finances and worried about their job security. I think we need to put on a happy face and let everyone know that we are in good shape and make the tough decisions ourselves. They don't need to be burdened with the challenges we are facing. We can carry that burden for them."

"I know you're trying to protect your colleagues from the harsh situation, Carl, but we have worked hard over the past year to build trust throughout the company with open and honest communications," John responded. "Now is not the time to pull back, but to communicate on a more frequent basis and to be available to respond to questions and concerns."

Transparency in communications is even more important in times of uncertainty. However, a natural reaction is to "hunker down," communicating only the more positive aspects of the situation to employees. In an attempt to protect employees, the organization, is undermining the trust of the workforce. The workforce knows or suspects there are significant issues facing the organization, and without information from leadership, they will fill the gaps with assumptions and inaccurate information. Rumors will become rampant. President and CEO of Nissan, Carlos Ghosn, credited with turning his company around, said, "One of the biggest signs that a company is in trouble is when the employees are confused about strategy and priorities."[3]

Ghosn also says this: "If you ask people to go through a difficult period of time, they have to trust that you're sharing it with them."[4] Now is exactly the time to reinforce the organization's mission and vision and provide a clear direction for the future. Reassure your team that a strategic plan exists to get the organization through the difficult period. Remind colleagues of previous challenges the organization has successfully navigated; share the human side through stories of those successes. Offer encouragement along the way by acknowledging and celebrating the small steps of progress and the incremental successes.

Resist a Command-and-Control Approach

"I've got nothing to work with here," observed Bill. "How are we supposed to lead the organization through this turnaround when we don't know for sure where we're going?"

"I'm so glad you asked that question." In seconds, John had typed a command on his laptop and the question appeared on the projection screen. "What do we know for sure?"

The next slide appeared, revealing the familiar words of the organization's mission statement.

"We know who we are," John commented.

The slide faded into a bulleted list of the organization's core values.

"And we know what's important."

"We know this, but I'm not sure how it helps in our current situation," said Rob.

"I can see why you might say that." John returned to his laptop, pressed a key, and four words began fading in and out slowly across the projection screen: Improvise, Adapt, Persist, Overcome.

"These are foundation words," John said. "These are the building blocks that will help us get through this time."

"I like these words," said Chip. "They sound strong and positive."

"They're action words," agreed Paul.

It is easy to revert to a more directive leadership approach in tough times. Leaders will often "put their nose to the grindstone" and bark orders with little more reason offered than "because I said so." While such an approach might seem to move things along more quickly, rarely does it work to garner the employees' enthusiasm and support. Discretionary efforts that were well-placed in the past will begin to crumble when employees no longer have the opportunity to share ideas and make meaningful contributions.

Instead, leaders should increase their visibility and place themselves in situations to listen to employees' thoughts, ideas, and opinions. "Being listened to is so close to being loved that most people cannot tell the difference," says David Oxberg.[5]

Chinese philosopher Lao Tzu, born circa 600 B.C., had this to say about leaders:

A leader is best

When people barely know that he exists,

Not so good when people obey and acclaim him,

Worst when they despise him.

"Fail to honor people,

They fail to honor you."

But of a good leader who talks little,

When his work is done, his aim fulfilled,

They will all say, "We did this ourselves."[6]

The Experience-versus-Potential Trap

John reached into a box on the floor near his chair, lifted up a long, slender stick and placed it on the table in front of him. Next, he reached back into the box, retrieved a handful of manila file folders, and handed them around to each person at the table. Curious, they glanced at each other, wondering what John had in store for them.

"I'm sure you're wondering why this is here," John said with a smile, pointing at the stick. "I wanted to see how many rainmakers we have in the room."

"Rainmakers?" Rita asked, confusion evident on her face.

John smiled. "Rainmakers. You know, high achievers that bring in new business and boost the work we're doing with our current clients." He nodded at the folders on the table. "I'd like each of you to take a look inside the folders in front of you," John replied. Opening the manila folders, each leader discovered a position description and two resumes inside, one labeled Candidate A and the other labeled Candidate B.

"I don't understand," said Chip. "Are we talking about revamping the HR department here?"

"I'd like you each to compare the two resumes in your folders," John responded. "What's your first inclination?"

"Well, at first glance, Candidate A looks pretty impressive," said Rob. "Solid education from a top school, several years of good experience, no gaps. Seems like a good fit for the position."

"I have some concerns about Candidate B," Rita commented. "I've never heard of this school, and the experience isn't all in our field. Looks like there are a couple of years unaccounted for, too."

"But I like the fact that Candidate B gives us this list of personal and professional highlights, even if they aren't all directly related to our field," pointed out Rob. "It seems like this person might have the aptitude to excel in this position, in spite of the educational and experience issues. Are these real applicants?"

"I've changed the names and positions to protect the innocent," John replied. "But these are resumes of people who actually work here already. Not necessarily people in this room, but people who are employed by this organization."

Glances were exchanged around the table as John continued.

"I'd like to talk with you a little bit about something called team selection," he explained. "I call it 'screening for ordinary greatness.' It's a bit nontraditional, but when it's used correctly,

(continued)

I've observed a dramatic increase in overall job satisfaction among new hires and a decrease in turnover, not just among new hires, but among existing employees."

"Okay, I'll bite—I'd like to know more," said Bill, leaning back in his chair.

"Well, the essence of it is this: Peers of prospective employees are inclined to look beyond the resume and evaluate the applicant's personality, attitude, and potential fit for the position," John explained. "We find that when we listen to people who know what it takes to perform a certain job, they're already tuned in to whether or not an applicant has the right combination of skills and traits to succeed in the position. And we found an unexpected benefit—when we ask staff members for their honest input and impressions, the fact that we listen to them and factor that into hiring decisions tells them 'we value you' in a big way. They're constantly looking to understand and define not just what they do, but what it takes to do it well."

"So this kind of challenge gets them focused on what's right, not what's wrong," Rita said slowly. "And it tells them their input really matters—they actually have some say in the kind of people that work next to them!"

"Precisely." John nodded, pleased. "It's not that education and experience aren't important. It's just that as we all know, people are made of far more than just their education and experience." He lifted the rainmaker, tilted it, and the room filled with a sound like flowing water. "Who wants to try being a rainmaker?"

Currently, the recruiting and hiring process has a fairly narrow focus. Human resource personnel are conditioned to rely on the proven experience and education set forth in a resume or curriculum vita. Potential aptitude, being an unknown variable, understandably carries less weight in the hiring process. What if these same professionals were coached to act as staffing rainmakers for the organization—to look beyond the degrees, awards, accomplishments, caliber of previous jobs, and screen for the "ordinary greatness" potential of an applicant?

Ricardo Semler, CEO of Semco, an industrial machinery firm, says it this way:

> Typical employee recruitment is like Internet dating. I'm always six foot four inches, and I look like Brad Pitt; you are always Cindy Crawford or Angelina Jolie. In the recruitment process, we put out fraudulent stuff about the company, like we're going to double our earnings, leaving out that we're also transferring all production to Vietnam in a year.
>
> You forget to tell us that you have fits of rage, that you worked six months here, six months there, and it's not on your resume. Then we meet at a bar and decide to marry. What are the chances that it's going to work?
>
> At Semco, we pick three candidates for further interviews. They'll come back several times. By the time we decide to marry, we know a lot about these people. That leaves us with 2 percent turnover in an industry with 18.[7]

One of the tools that helps organizations guard against the experience-versus-potential trap is a team selection process to identify the best person for an open position. Essentially, no one is hired without feedback from potential peers—no one. Why? It is too easy to default to the person possessing a resume documenting an impressive educational background and experience. But while these factors are important, there are other aspects that must be considered. We find that front-line staff and peers will look beyond the standard resume to choose the best candidate. They evaluate the personality, attitude, and all-important "fit" of the person. The result is a decrease in employee turnover, higher employee satisfaction, and enhanced teamwork.

A paradigm shift is in order for organizations that want to attract, hire, and retain people whose potential is just as impressive as their overt skills. Here's an example:

A young man dropped out of Reed College in Portland, Oregon, the Northwest's premier liberal arts college and went back home. Some time later, the 18-year-old applied for a job at a local plant. The personnel director went into the office of the operations leader and told him that he had an applicant determined to go to work for them, so

set on getting a job that he refused to leave without talking to someone higher in the chain of command.

So the young man got his interview and subsequently was hired.
Why? He so impressed the manager with his determined attitude, inner
energy, and vision that his lack of education and experience were not
deterrents. Instead, his potential for greatness was recognized.

The company was Atari, and the college dropout was Steve Jobs,
founder of Apple.[8]

Take Advantage of Opportunities

Pleased with the conversation, John pressed a computer key
and another slide appeared on the screen.

"Leadership is the art of getting someone else to do
something you want done because they want to do it."

– Dwight Eisenhower

"So we're back to how to motivate our staff?" Bill asked.
"I think we motivate our staff members by giving them a
voice, and reminding them that ultimately, they need to support
and respect decisions made for the good of the whole company." John glanced around the table. "Great leaders look out
for their people. And you know what? You're great leaders!"

Whether it is with people, products, services, or finances, there are
countless opportunities to provide a competitive advantage or set the
company up for future success. A notable example is the contrast in
approaches between two electronics retailers, Circuit City and Best Buy.
In 2007, Circuit City cut the jobs of 3,400 of its top-paid sales associates
as it was on the verge of implementing a massive effort to transform
its customer experience and revive sales. Needless to say, without the

knowledge and experience of these key employees, the transformation effort failed. Within a year Circuit City's sales were continuing a downward spiral, and its stock had declined more than 75% in value. During that same time period, Circuit City's competitor, Best Buy, took advantage of a market opportunity, added specially trained staff, and realized a 52% increase in profits. Fast forward to early 2009, when Circuit City announced it would close all stores after failing to find a buyer for the company; by March 2009, the company had shut down completely. While there were certainly other significant factors involved in the demise of Circuit City, the decision to reduce the workforce and specifically to eliminate the high performers' jobs eliminated the potential that existed for these individuals to assist in developing and implementing strategies that might have saved the company.[9]

Elevate Your Focus on Encouraging Ordinary Greatness

"This may seem to be coming from left field, but I think we have an opportunity here to do some additional training and development and prepare our workforce for our new reality," said Rita. "In fact, if we're smart, we can design a talent management initiative that gets us ahead of the curve."

"What do you mean?" asked Carl.

"Well, it's a matter of demonstrating our belief that our people are our greatest resource. Let's equip them with new knowledge and skills that will put them at the forefront of this new economic environment."

"That's exactly the type of leadership thinking I know I can count on you to provide," replied John. "Let's review our notes from last year's Talent Management Summit and identify opportunities to reposition some of our employees to better align with the revised organizational structure."

Toyota is masterful in taking advantage of opportunities, especially in leveraging its talent. Toyota Motor Company is experiencing the same downturn as its counterparts in the automotive industry. But unlike its competitors, Toyota has made a commitment to keep full-time employees even in the face of significant reductions in assembly-line production. These assembly-line workers are deployed to training classes, where they can hone their quality control and productivity knowledge and skills. Jim Lentz, president of Toyota Motor Sales, the company's U.S. sales unit, said the company believes keeping employees on the payroll and using the time to improve their capabilities is the best move in the long run. "It would have been crazy for us to lose people for 90 days and (then) to rehire and retrain people and hope that we have a smooth ramp-up coming back in," Lentz said. Toyota believes in its people and actively finds ways to identify and leverage the ordinary greatness in the workforce. In turn, the employees are energized and committed to helping the company reach its goals. As one worker put it, "One of the major things that everyone is grateful for is that they thought enough of us to keep us here."[10]

Call in the Reinforcements

"I'd like to propose something," John said quietly.

Everyone leaned in.

"I'd like to call a family meeting."

"A what?" Chip asked.

"Well, if we tell our staff members to treat our customers like family, why shouldn't we treat each other the same way?"

"Interesting. Please continue," said Chip.

"During times like these, I don't think it works to try and pretend it's business as usual. I don't think our staff needs a heavy-handed approach with lots of rigid guidelines and procedure enforcement. What if we actually acknowledge the elephant in the room—the situation as it really is and as it could be if things don't turn around soon?" John paused to let his words sink in.

"Wouldn't that just add to everyone's stress?" Rita asked.

"Think how stressful it is to try and evaluate a situation objectively when you don't have enough information to make a decision," John pointed out. "I'm not saying to turn ourselves completely inside out, although transparency is one of our core values! But what if we gave our staff enough information that they could evaluate the issues and maybe even offer some possible solutions?"

"That just might work," Bill said.

"I know how important it is to feel like someone's really listening to me and valuing my input," said Rita. "When they're receptive to my suggestions . . ."

"It builds a stronger team."

"What if we formed teams to address specific issues?"

"How do we keep them from getting out of control?"

"I don't see the word 'control' on the screen."

"This involves a huge risk. What if it backfires?"

"Then we re-evaluate and try another approach."

Tom Rohrs, CEO of Electroglas, said, "One of the best ways to get through a downturn is to have a firm understanding and belief that there's going to be an upturn."[11] Challenging times can bring out the best or the worst in leaders. Make it the best by focusing on reinforcing the vision for the future, enhancing communications, and involving others in making the tough decisions. Now is the time to approach your business with fresh eyes. Determine the critical processes and practices that will grow and sustain your business. Face the brutal realities of those processes and practices that no longer drive value. Determine new approaches, products, or services that will create a competitive advantage. Listen to your customers—they will reveal the answers. Listen to your staff—they will help make it happen. Organizations need to call upon the ordinary greatness that exists in their organizations. It will set your organization apart and move you into a future full of possibilities.

John Kenneth Galbraith said, "All of the great leaders have had one characteristic in common: The willingness to confront the major anxiety of their people in their time. This, and not much else, is the essence of leadership."[12]

Challenging times can bring out the best or the worst in leaders.

- How are you laying the groundwork for success during these challenging times?
- What can you do personally to promote an open mindset when change is occurring?
- What are the leadership basics that you adhere to that cannot be compromised when times get tough?

Closing Comments

As divine intervention would have it, we had the opportunity to spend some time chatting with close friend and mentor Lance Secretan as we were frantically completing the manuscript for this book. We spoke of our sense of a different world with different needs and different priorities; a new framework for the 21st century. It is a framework Lance recounts in his most recent work on leadership, *One: The Art and Practice of Conscious Leadership.*[1] His theory of a new vision—"a vision of reconnecting each of us with our deepest human needs"—offers obvious parallels to our work on ordinary greatness.

We talked a great deal about the greatness we see in our own lives, the lessons we have learned from observing greatness in others, and the possibilities that lie ahead. The conversation eventually turned to what each of us had viewed earlier in the day: the telecast of the inauguration of our 44th President, Barack Obama. Our new President symbolized the possibilities that can become reality when blinders are removed. His message that day rang with hope and inspiration. His words spoke to our hearts and reflected this theme of ordinary greatness:

> In reaffirming the greatness of our nation, we understand that greatness is never a given. It must be earned. Our journey has

157

never been one of shortcuts or settling for less. It has not been the path for the fainthearted, for those that prefer leisure over work, or seek only the pleasures of riches and fame. Rather, it has been the risk-takers, the doers, the makers of things—some celebrated, but more often men and women obscure in their labor—who have carried us up the long, rugged path towards prosperity and freedom.[2]

We started this book by presenting a scene of a crowded Metro station with people too busy to notice greatness where they had not expected to see it. Throughout the book, we have challenged leaders to be aware of the blinders, to be more open to the greatness all around them, and to go through each day ready to provide a spark that will become the light that illuminates and attracts ordinary greatness. But there is always the nagging feeling at the end of a book like this that it still will not be enough. That people will continue to be more focused on getting through the turnstiles than on seeing the greatness that is right before them.

Over the months that we wrote the book, as we watched the economic downturn, talked to corporate leaders, and read the various articles written since the beginning of 2009 about the new expectations for the business world, we came to a realization that this time it is different. The old "get all you can, can all you get, and sit on the lid" mentality of go-go consumption seems faded and even a bit grotesque. It seems that we are replacing this jaded philosophy with a simpler, more focused way of life, one that requires thoughtfulness and social responsibility, volunteerism, and an awareness that "every village matters," as former Secretary of State Colin Powell stated. Not to say it is not scary—it is. Perhaps now is the first time in history when a book like this with a message like this can actually make a difference. Perhaps now this music will be heard.

Are you listening?

APPENDIX A

Assessments

In efforts to maximize our potential and the potential of those we lead, it is critical that we take time to reflect upon leadership concepts and areas of personal growth. Throughout the book, we have challenged your current thinking and actions with questions at the end of each chapter. We have provided an opportunity for you to delve a bit deeper by offering the following self-assessments.

The Personal Blinders Assessment (Exhibit A.1) is based on the material found in Chapter 3, "Why People Do Not See Ordinary Greatness" and Chapter 4, "How Leaders Open Their Eyes to Ordinary Greatness." We recommend that you review these chapters once you have completed the assessment to gain a greater understanding of how the blinders impede your ability to see and act upon ordinary greatness. If you would like a personalized analysis and recommended strategies for overcoming your blinders, please go to www.ordinarygreatnessbook.com.

The How You View the World Assessment (Exhibit A.2) indicates your propensity for recognizing, appreciating, celebrating, and promoting ordinary greatness based on how you tend to respond to daily life. This assessment expands the concepts introduced in Chapter 9, "Changing the

Way You View the World." You can also go to www.ordinarygreatnessbook
.com to take this as an online survey and receive a complimentary analysis.
Your password is "greatness."

Remember: Everything you need to be successful currently exists
in your workforce. Open your eyes to the ordinary greatness that can
propel you and your organization to extraordinary heights.

Personal Blinders
Assessment
Please fill in the box next to the response that best represents your answer.
5 = always; **4** = usually; **3** = sometimes; **2** = rarely; **1** = never

1. Do you get your impression of the work environment from
   first-hand experience instead of what people tell you is occurring?
   5☐ 4☐ 3☐ 2☐ 1☐

2. Are you hesitant to support new ways of approaching workplace
   issues?
   5☐ 4☐ 3☐ 2☐ 1☐

3. Do you know what motivates your staff?
   5☐ 4☐ 3☐ 2☐ 1☐

4. Do you believe that an individual's discretionary effort directly
   reflects their level of commitment?
   5☐ 4☐ 3☐ 2☐ 1☐

5. Do you visit work areas on a consistent basis to establish
   relationships with your colleagues and open lines of communication?
   5☐ 4☐ 3☐ 2☐ 1☐

6. Is your opinion of others influenced by what you hear?
   5☐ 4☐ 3☐ 2☐ 1☐

7. Are you able to link what employees do on a daily basis to the
   success of the organization?
   5☐ 4☐ 3☐ 2☐ 1☐

8. Is your daily work a check-the-box kind of existence, consumed
   with doing tasks rather than being available for others?
   5☐ 4☐ 3☐ 2☐ 1☐

9. Do you avoid making judgment of a person based on their
   personal appearance?
   5☐ 4☐ 3☐ 2☐ 1☐

10. Do your own biases about a person's background, race, or
    gender lead you to make assumptions about his/her abilities?
    5☐ 4☐ 3☐ 2☐ 1☐

Exhibit A.1   Personal Blinders assessment

Please fill in the box next to the response that best represents your answer.
5 = always; **4** = usually; **3** = sometimes; **2** = rarely; **1** = never

11. Does the ability to relate to others' ideas and opinions come easily to you?

    5☐   4☐   3☐   2☐   1☐

12. Do you believe certain people will never exhibit high performance?

    5☐   4☐   3☐   2☐   1☐

13. Do your colleagues consider you to be approachable?

    5☐   4☐   3☐   2☐   1☐

14. Is it difficult for you to envision an employee working outside their area of expertise?

    5☐   4☐   3☐   2☐   1☐

15. Are you open to others' opinions, even if they differ from your own?

    5☐   4☐   3☐   2☐   1☐

16. Are you quick to jump to conclusions based on your previous experiences?

    5☐   4☐   3☐   2☐   1☐

17. Are you supportive of everyone, regardless of their current level of performance?

    5☐   4☐   3☐   2☐   1☐

18. Are you addicted to schedules and calendars that leave limited room for personal connections?

    5☐   4☐   3☐   2☐   1☐

19. Do you encourage staff development and foster participation in learning opportunities?

    5☐   4☐   3☐   2☐   1☐

20. Is it difficult to overcome your first impression of a situation, no matter what evidence is presented?

    5☐   4☐   3☐   2☐   1☐

Proceed to next page to calculate your results.

Exhibit A.1   (Continued)

Personal Bias

1. + ☐
6. − ☐
11. + ☐
16. − ☐
    = ☐

Preconceived Notions

2. − ☐
3. + ☐
12. − ☐
17. + ☐
    = ☐

Busyness

5. + ☐
8. − ☐
13. + ☐
18. − ☐
    = ☐

Compartmentalization

4. − ☐
7. + ☐
14. − ☐
19. + ☐
    = ☐

External Focus

9. + ☐
10. − ☐
15. + ☐
20. − ☐
    = ☐

Transfer the number scored for each question on the grid below. Total each column, adding and subtracting as indicated.

A score of 3 or lower indicates that this particular blinder is preventing you from fully recognizing the ordinary greatness that exists in your personal and professional life. Your acknowledgment of the blinder is the first step to eliminating its impact.

A score of 4 or greater indicates that the blinder is not significantly affecting your ability to identify ordinary greatness. You should continue to be aware of the various blinders and guard against any negative impact they may have.

Exhibit A.1   (Continued)

How You View the World
Assessment

Is every moment of your day scheduled?

☐ a. Absolutely; I have no time for spontaneous opportunities that come along

☐ b. Pretty much; only small windows of unscheduled time are available

☐ c. Not so much; I have flexibility in my schedule

☐ d. Not at all; I have a very loose schedule

Would you strike up a conversation with a stranger?

☐ a. Never; I am intimidated by strangers

☐ b. Rarely; I am cautious around strangers

☐ c. Sometimes; I might, given the right opportunities

☐ d. Always; I love the process of getting acquainted with others

Do you try new things?

☐ a. Rarely; I prefer to stick to things I am familiar with

☐ b. Sometimes; it takes a push from someone to get me to try new things

☐ c. Often; I am okay with "selected" adventures

☐ d. Always; I love to experience everything new and different

Do you learn a new skill or talent each year?

☐ a. No, I tend to build on what I already know

☐ b. Maybe, but it is usually forced upon me

☐ c. Sometimes I get a "wild hare" and commit to learning something new

☐ d. I plan to learn something new each year

Exhibit A.2   How You View the World assessment

Do you read at least six books a year?

- ❏ a. No, not even close
- ❏ b. On average, I read 1-3 books each year
- ❏ c. On average, I read 4-6 books each year
- ❏ d. I read more than 6 books every year

Do you surround yourself with people who think differently than you?

- ❏ a. No, I prefer to be around people that have my same views
- ❏ b. Rarely, and only when the circumstance demands it
- ❏ c. It happens, but not easily and not without a reason
- ❏ d. Yes, I love to hear different approaches and ideas

Are your best friends carbon copies of you?

- ❏ a. Yes, we have the same background, experiences, and interests
- ❏ b. Most are, although there are a few exceptions
- ❏ c. It's a mix of those with similar backgrounds and interests and those who have different backgrounds and interests
- ❏ d. No, I am most attracted to people who are different from me

Are you a risk-taker?

- ❏ a. Absolutely not, I take the safe option every time
- ❏ b. Only when forced to take a risk, either by circumstance or by others
- ❏ c. Sometimes, but only after carefully weighing the risk and determining that there is a relatively good chance of things working out in my favor
- ❏ d. Yes, I love the thrill and excitement of "going for it"

Do you look for the lesson in each experience?

- ❏ a. I have to admit that I don't look at life that way
- ❏ b. Yes, if it's pretty profound and apparent
- ❏ c. On occasion, I stop to consider what the experience has taught me
- ❏ d. I always reflect on what I have learned from each experience

Exhibit A.2   (Continued)

**Do you make your passions a priority
in your life?**

☐ a. I am not really sure what I am passionate about, other than
        my family
☐ b. I rarely find the time or energy to devote to my passions
☐ c. I do spend some time, but not enough, on my passions
☐ d. I make sure that I devote myself to my passions

**Calculate the number of responses in each
category and multiply as instructed:**

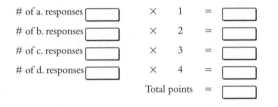

# of a. responses [＿＿]   ×   1   = [＿＿]

# of b. responses [＿＿]   ×   2   = [＿＿]

# of c. responses [＿＿]   ×   3   = [＿＿]

# of d. responses [＿＿]   ×   4   = [＿＿]

                              Total points = [＿＿]

If you scored 0–10: By virtue of your thoughts and actions, you
        are prevented from seeing everyday greatness that exists
        right in front of you, as well as the potential for greatness in
        yourself and others.

If you scored 11–20: While you have several areas of
        enlightened thinking and behaving, you only see a portion
        of the greatness that exists in your world.

If you scored 21–30: You have a tendency to recognize
        greatness in the heroic and in the everyday actions of
        others.

If you scored 31–40: You are not only open to observing,
        appreciating, and recognizing ordinary greatness, you find
        great joy in its discovery and celebration.

Exhibit A.2   (Continued)

APPENDIX B

Questions and Answers

The following are examples of questions we have received that relate to the ideas and concepts found in *Ordinary Greatness*.

Getting the Boss to Buy In

Q: I believe in the concepts of ordinary greatness, but my boss just doesn't get it, and sees no value in being visible, communicating, and spotting ordinary greatness. What do I do?

A: Thank you so much for this question. It is one that we have heard more than once, and when it is asked, we always take it seriously, because we have all been there at least once. Unfortunately, there are still leaders who, despite having read books and gained knowledge, just do not seem to get it.

Here are our suggestions:

- First of all, keep in mind that people can change. None of us were born practicing these leadership behaviors. We have all had mentors and role models who showed us how we would have to change. Stay positive regarding your boss. Keep control of your emotions. Do not let frustration or hatefulness enter the picture.

- After that, ask yourself whether you are doing everything that you can, and for which you do not need permission, to find and develop ordinary greatness. Some people, when they see the boss not buying in, get frustrated, and say, "When the boss does it, then I will. When the boss is visible, then I will be. When the boss recognizes me for my great work, then I will recognize my staff." This is just about the worst approach, for now we have *two* leaders who are not following through, and the negative impact on staff is at least doubled. Are you doing everything in your zone of responsibility to promote ordinary greatness? If your boss *did* buy in, how would you behave differently? Remember, *you are responsible for your outcomes*. Are you being visible? Are you recognizing? Are you spotting ordinary greatness in your staff? You probably do not need the boss's permission to be positive, remove blinders, and have aspirational conversations with staff. It is difficult, but take ownership. Hey, if it were easy, everyone would be doing it, right? But the hard things are where the greatest learning occurs. We often tell our clients to overrule their instincts. Who do you not want to talk to? This is probably who you should talk to today. What task do you not want to do? This is probably what you should do first. It is difficult, but take ownership. Jim Collins summed it up:

Do you believe that your ultimate outcomes in life are externally determined—I came from a certain family, I got the right job? Or do you believe that how your life turns out is ultimately up to you, that despite all the things that happen, you are ultimately responsible for your outcomes?

Consider the airline industry, and think of all the events and factors outside managerial control that have hit it since 1972: fuel shocks, interest rate spikes, deregulation, wars, and 9/11. And yet the number-one performing company of all publicly traded companies in terms of return to investors for a 30-year period from 1972 to 2002 is an airline. According to *Money* magazine's retrospective look in 2002, Southwest Airlines beat Intel, Walmart,

GE—all of them! Now what would have happened if the folks at Southwest had said, "Hey, we can't do anything great because of our environment?" You could say, "Yeah, the airline industry is terrible. Everyone in it is statistically destined to lose money." But at Southwest they say, "We are responsible for our own outcomes."[1]

- Next, remember it is possible to lead your boss. It may be incumbent on you to teach your boss how to spot ordinary greatness. Those of us with children know that our kids have taught us some great lessons. What lessons will you teach your boss? Here are some practical tips for teaching your boss how to spot ordinary greatness:
  - Invite your boss to tour the work area with you, engaging staff along the way.
  - Every Friday, before you leave for home, send the boss an e-mail or voicemail telling him the greatest thing that your employees did that week, along with a recommended time to stop by and thank them.
  - If you have a meeting with your boss coming up, tell your staff and ask them if there is anything they would like to pass along.
  - Caution: Do not "throw your boss under the bus" to staff. Avoid making negative comments about your boss in front of your staff. While this might feel like you are fitting in with staff at that moment, you are only undermining your own leadership.
- Finally, if your boss will not change, and the situation becomes untenable, you might have to find a new boss. Life is too short and our window to make a difference too small to waste time with those who will never match our worldview and values. You might wind up being more successful somewhere else, but we have seen that many leaders do not have to take that step.

Hang in there—you can make a difference!

Motivating Beyond the Minimum

Q: I understand the concepts of mandatory and discretionary effort, and it is certainly at play in my department. I have a core group of top performers who give more than is required, yet I also have a small group of poor performers who give just the minimum and seem immune to all of my efforts to motivate them. Help!

A: Your question is evidence that, while consultants and authors can make it seem easy, implementing the ordinary greatness principles in real-life situations is anything but. Here are some strategies to use to make it, if not easy, maybe easier.

First of all, remember to keep your perspective. While it certainly seems that the poor performers are taking up most of your time and effort, they are not your entire staff.

Our goal is to get to the point where most of our time is spent with top performers. They are the ones our customers love most, who have the most career options (so they are the most at-risk to leave), and who can make your life easier. Shower them with recognition, greater responsibilities, and constant coaching. Interesting point: Managers rarely have to ask for help in identifying top performers. Even in work situations where there are few or no evaluation tools available, managers seem to know who the top performers are and who the laggards are. They just do.

That being said, you must deal with your poor performers, too. As we learned in our discussion of the Tator Principle, poor performers with negative attitudes can be isolated, but their attitudes must be addressed at some point. We are often tempted to put off these difficult situations, or we may fool ourselves into thinking things are improving because "I haven't heard anything lately." Wrong. In this case, no news is not good news. Remember, you will often be the last to know about things that occur in the department, because many people will not want to tell the boss about the performance of others. They would rather not be involved. As a student of history, I (Brian) have seen this lesson proved in the lives of historical figures. For example, around the time of the American Revolution, many British politicians felt this rebellion was just a phase that would pass. Until the pitchforks and torches appear over the hills, the leader is often clueless. Do not neglect to act proactively.

Failure to deal with poor performers can be deadly to your career. Leaders who are not willing to coach or move along underperformers place themselves in danger of the following outcomes:

- Colleagues notice when you do not deal with poor performers, which is how reputations are formed. If you do not coach or move along your poor performers, your peers will notice, and they will lose respect for you. We all know leaders who coach and leaders who do not. How do you want to be remembered?

- The top performers notice whether a leader coaches and holds people accountable, and the top performers quickly lose regard for the leader who does not follow through with holding poor performers accountable. The top performers talk to top performers from other parts of the company, and they tell the others what kind of leader their boss is. Do you want to be viewed as the career destination for the best and brightest in your company?
- Your valuable time and energy are wasted in trying to change people who might not be willing to change, and your quality of life suffers.
- You get so frustrated that you start to take this out on your top performers. We have all seen this at home. After a tough day at work, we are tempted to "go off" on our family members. They are innocent, but in the wrong place at the wrong time. This situation is regrettable, but we do it at work as well. If your staff has to ask each other, "What kind of mood is he/she in?" then work is needed in this area.

Now that you are convinced of the need to deal with poor performers, how should it be done? A great place to start is with a clearly written plan of goals, objectives, and outcomes. List the key outcomes for the staff, and ask each staff member to contribute action steps to which each can commit that will help accomplish a goal. For example, if one of the goals is that 90% of phone calls be answered without rolling to voicemail, one of the action steps could be the development of some consistent word choices to excuse themselves from an ongoing interaction so they can get to the phone. The key point is to get the staff member involved in your plan for improvement, without doing it for them. A common mistake at this stage is to take over and do everything for the staff member. In this way, the manager has taken all of the accountability, and the poor performer is let off the hook once again. Keep the accountability where it belongs.

Once things are clearly listed on paper, meet at least monthly to go over results and improvement areas. But do not wait for a monthly meeting. If performance needs to be addressed, do it now! Never make a staff member guess where he or she stands with you. Guessing is our enemy; clarity is our friend. Our goal is to make evaluation day the most boring, anticlimactic day of the year, because, in essence, we have been having it every day.

While you are giving clear, honest feedback to all staff members (not just poor performers, but that is the topic of this Q&A), remember to stay positive and upbeat. You own your mood. Stay in control.

At this point, results and outcomes are in the hands of the poor performer. You may have to ask the staff member to leave the company, but often this outcome is not necessary. In many cases, the poor performer is turned off by the coaching, clarity, and accountability, and they may leave voluntarily, to everyone's relief.

Bottom line: *Act.*

What would you do if you were not afraid?

What would you do if you knew you could not fail?

The answers to these questions probably contain your next course of action.

Discovering the Root Cause of Low Performance

Q: As a seasoned leader, I understand how important it is to recognize people for doing a great job. But I have to admit that I am finding it more and more difficult to see "greatness" in the individual and team efforts in my division. It seems to me that the vast majority of staff is performing at a mediocre level, doing what needs to be done but not stretching themselves to do their best work. I do not want to encourage the continuation of this level of performance by recognizing individuals or teams who are not performing at the highest level. What other engagement strategies would you suggest?

A: There are two concepts that are important to address in this response. First, it is important to understand why the performance level is subpar. If the specific skills to successfully perform the work are present, you have to ask yourself several questions. Is there a lack of clarity regarding performance expectations? Does each member of your staff relate his or her work to the strategies driving your division's success? If the answer to either or both of these questions is negative, those may be some of the reasons you observe staff putting the time, but not the passion or energy into their work. They are confused about which items need their focused attention, or they simply cannot connect how their work makes a difference, both of which lead to disengagement and low performance.

If, however, you find that expectations are clear and people are able to connect their daily work with business results, then you need to look further. Is it a communication issue? Are you encouraging others to excel? Have you removed any barriers that would prevent the staff from doing their best work?

The second concept is to challenge your observation that greatness does not exist in your division. Psychiatrist R.D. Lang offers some words of wisdom: "The range of what we think and do is limited by what we fail to notice. And because we fail to notice that we fail to notice, there is little we can do to change, until we notice how failing to notice shapes our thoughts and deeds."[2] Is it possible that you are wearing a set of blinders that keep you from recognizing those who are truly engaged and doing exceptional work? Is it your mindset that is creating the perception of mediocrity? In other words, are you expecting mediocre performance, ensuring that you see mediocre performance? Would your perception change if you were expecting greatness at every turn? No doubt the communication, encouragement, and inspiration you provide would be different.

Finally, I would encourage you not to abandon recognition as an engagement strategy. While I certainly would not suggest that you use recognition when the recognition is not deserved, it is a powerful way to reinforce those behaviors you want to see throughout the division. Adjust your definition of greatness beyond the monumental, overt successes so that you are not overlooking the ordinary, everyday contributions that individuals and the team consistently make.

Rediscovering Your Passion

Q: What should I do if I feel I have lost my passion? When I started in this job as an HR director at a Fortune 500 company, I was excited to go to work every day, and I was genuinely thrilled at the prospect of serving and helping so many people. But now, three years later,

that all seems a distant memory. My days are now filled with boring policy and procedure reviews, endless meetings, and a boss I hate.
With this economy, I am terrified to even think about leaving. Help!

A: Thank you for your question. I wish yours was the only "I've lost
my passion" question we received, but unfortunately, it was not.

This feeling of lost passion is sapping our people, hurting our bottom
line, and postponing our eventual recovery from this economic mess. The
greatest waste in American business is not office supplies, buildings, or
even salaries. The greatest waste is occurring every day, anytime someone leaves work feeling that they could have given more, been more
passionate, or been more engaged. What is standing in the way of our
giving more? Maybe we gave lots of discretionary effort once, and no
one seemed to notice or care. Maybe we went the extra mile with a customer, but our attentiveness was repaid with rudeness. Regardless, it is
critical to get back the passion!

First, start hanging out and associating with passionate people.
Who are your mentors and close associates? Are they positive, reasonable people who take their passion with them, or are they part of the
crowd that complains, sees mostly the negative, and moans about
the job and top leadership? Be sure your friends and associates are
people who do their best to live the "five positives for every negative"
rule. Just as you guard your children's associations, guard your own professional associations. Some people are energy and passion drainers, and
you do not have time to deal with them. Abandon them with kindness
and grace. You will be glad you did. Find the most passionate people
you know and spend the most time with them. Find the people that, as
Mike Rowe said, take their passion with them everywhere they go.

In every interaction, go the extra mile. And if you cannot feel the
passion? Then, as one boss used to tell me, "Fake it 'til you make it.
The customer won't care—they'll be glad to have the service." By the
way, do you know where that phrase "go the extra mile" comes from?
Legend has it that when the ancient Romans would conquer a new
land, they would sometimes create a requirement that any conquered
civilian must carry a Roman soldier's gear for one mile. That was the
law. One mile. But going beyond that, and carrying it for another mile,
an extra mile, was not the law. That was doing it for love.

Early in my career, I (Brian) worked in HR at a hospital that required its employees to, if we saw someone lost in the hallway, stop, introduce ourselves, and offer to take them where they needed to go. One day, I was walking through the hospital, late for a meeting (as usual), when I saw a man, obviously lost. You know they are lost when they are staring at the ceiling with a blank look on their face. He was also carrying a Winnie the Pooh gift bag with colorful tissue paper coming out of it—it was obviously a gift for a new baby or a new mother. Seeing this man, and knowing where he needed to go, I knew what would happen if I followed my employer's requirement and took him to the Mother/Baby Unit. It was way out of my way, and I would be even later to my meeting. What should I do?

Well, being terrified of someone seeing me not do the right thing, I approached the man, introduced myself, and offered to escort him where he was headed. He told me, "Thanks. My name is Pat, and I just flew here from San Diego. I'm here to welcome my first grandchild into the world!"

Wow—talk about getting your passion back. I almost missed the best part about working in a hospital—getting to share this kind of joy. Pat did not care why I helped him, he was just glad to get the help, and I lived off sharing this sweet moment with him for days. Forget the meeting, I was making a difference!

To get your passion back, ask yourself, whom can I make a difference with today? Who needs me?

In this situation, there is no greater role model than Homer Simpson, who learned the answer to this question in *The Simpsons* episode "And Maggie Makes Three," from the sixth season of the television program. In this episode, Homer tells Bart and Lisa the story surrounding the birth of their younger sister Maggie.

Homer said that he originally was not that thrilled about the prospect of another child, and he was completely unenthusiastic about the impending birth. Homer had just taken his dream job at a bowling alley, but because of the growth of his family, he would have to go to his old boss, Mr. Burns, and beg for his job back. Not easy, because he had (literally) burned some bridges. Of course, Mr. Burns did make Homer beg for his job back, and placed a large plaque in front of Homer's desk reading: "*Don't forget: You're here forever.*" Naturally, as soon as he saw Maggie for the first time, Homer got his "daddy passion" back. Homer then answers Bart and Lisa's question, "Why don't we have any baby pictures of Maggie?" by telling them that he keeps those pictures in the place where he needs them the most. The scene then cuts to his workplace where all of the Maggie photos are positioned on the wall around the plaque, which now reads: "*Do it for her.*"[3]

Who are you passionate about? Who are you doing all this for? Find your passion and take it with you!

Strategizing for Talent Management

Q: As the new chief operating officer (COO) of a telecommunications firm, I am concerned that our talent management strategy will not carry us into the future with the skills and knowledge needed to be successful. Currently Human Resources owns this initiative and handles all aspects of implementing the program, from selection of high-potential leaders to development of the training curriculum for all employees. In my last organization, the talent management strategy was more fully deployed among the leadership group. Which is the right way to go?

A: Kudos to you. It is obvious from your question that you know something about the importance of a solid talent management strategy. I also commend you for placing it high on your list of priorities for review. Talent management, or "Talent Greatness," as we call it in *Ordinary Greatness,* is critical to preparing your organization's workforce for the challenges ahead.

Your concern about ownership of the talent strategy is one I wish more executives would consider. A common mistake we see in the design and implementation of a talent management strategy is the belief that it is solely the purview of the human resources department. Too often we hear managers say "It's HR's job" when it comes to identifying, developing, and retaining employees. And all too often, HR agrees. Don't get me wrong, human resources has a critical role in ensuring the success of any talent management initiative and should lead the process. However, without a viable partnership with the organization's management staff, the support for a robust talent management initiative wavers.

The reality is that the majority (60%) of managers believe that HR is an administrative department and not a strategic partner, as cited in a recent study by McKinsey & Company. Further, the study indicated that 58% of managers surveyed felt HR lacks the capability to develop a talent strategy aligned to the organization's business objectives.[4]

An important step in elevating your talent management program is to form a partnership between HR and the organization's leaders and managers. A series of open discussion sessions on your organization's future talent needs, programmatic approaches to developing and retaining talent, and defined roles and responsibilities of HR as well as managers will go a long way in forming an aligned partnership that works together in supporting this important strategy. One best practice we have seen work well is the formation of ongoing advisory groups with representatives from HR, senior leaders, and line managers. Advisory groups based on functional areas such as recruitment, retention, development, and other high-potential programs tap into the ideas of a diverse group and create the endorsement and support necessary for the successful implementation of these types of programs. The members of these advisory groups become your best advocates and signify that a partnership exists and all viewpoints are heard.

Finally, it is important that your approach to managing your talent be closely linked to your organization's strategic priorities. This alignment will ensure that your talent initiatives are not working at odds with other business strategies and are instead supportive and complementary. Not only should you have a current talent inventory identifying gaps that need to be filled in the short term, you must be forward-thinking and identify the skills and knowledge needs of the future.

Keeping Top Performers Motivated

Q: I have top performers on my staff whom I fear are becoming bored. How do I keep them engaged so they continue to be top performers, stay with the company, and perhaps even succeed me when I retire in a few years?

A: Congratulations on spotting ordinary greatness in your staff members. Employers like you truly inspire all of us to do great things every day.

The best tip for you is to purposely look for development opportunities for these top performers. This will not happen by accident. If you wait, it might be too late. Ensure that the ongoing aspirational conversations you have with them define specific actions to help them grow. Here are some examples:

- Is there outside coaching or development that could be made available?
- Can you provide greater access to your boss and/or Board of Directors? If one of them may be your successor, for the good of your company and your customers, perhaps they should get acquainted now.
- Are there classes this person could teach, or is there some way in which their knowledge and experience can be shared with others? The opportunity to teach and develop others might be just what is needed to keep them engaged and on the job.
- What "stretch assignments" are available? You should not protect your top performers from bigger, more important projects. In fact, remove trivial tasks that anyone can do, and give them the big stuff to work on with you. We often hear, "If you want something done, give it to the busiest person on the team." True. Some people just have a greater capacity for work and manage to get more done. Watch out for burnout, though, and ask frequently about workload and work/life balance. Our goal is to keep people fascinated and energized at work, not make their lives unmanageable.
- Can you "loan" these staff members to a key supplier or customer? What they learn while gaining some fresh perspective in another industry or part of the business could be the best investment ever.
- Look for an important community effort for this staff member to lead. Whether taking the lead on building a Habitat for Humanity house, collecting coats for the homeless, or assisting with a United Way drive, let your community share in this person's excellence. Win, win, win!

Finding Time for Ordinary Greatness

Q: Help! I just do not have time to spot ordinary greatness in my staff. I'm crazy busy. My day is one endless stream of meetings and firefighting.

A: Please, do not feel bad or be too hard on yourself. Most leaders are in this spot, and in these times of cutbacks and "do more with less," it will only get worse.

There are no easy answers, but here are some practical tips that might help you have a little more time to spot ordinary greatness:

- Audit every e-mail list to which you subscribe, every meeting you attend, and every team of which you are a member, and ask some honest questions. Does this activity add value to me, my staff, or my customers? If not, it may be expendable. Abandon it.

- Stop attending meetings that your staff also attend. We are not talking about staff meetings you call and lead. We are referring to regular, interdisciplinary company meetings we find ourselves pulled into. If you are there with your staff, one of you is not necessary. Remember, the highest ranking person in the room will always be accountable for whatever has to be done after the meeting, so your staff might view your presence as "protection." Instead, tell your staff member to go ahead and attend the meeting while you go do something *only you can do* (be visible, recognize other staff members, remove barriers, spot ordinary greatness). Then say something like, "Thank you for attending this meeting. Before you leave today, can you send me a note listing what was discussed (clarity), who is going to do what (commitments), and what the communication plan is (cascading)." The staff member will feel more accountable and will pay close attention.

- If a staff member comes to you and says something like, "Boss, we've got a problem," instead of taking immediate ownership of the issue for the staff member, listen to their description of the issue and then ask them to send you a note briefly describing the issue along with two or three of their ideas for solving the issue and what they need from you. This will save you time, keep the accountability where it belongs, and teach ownership principles to your staff. Then you can recognize and thank them for showing ordinary greatness when they solve the issue.

- Be less accessible. This book has encouraged visibility, but do not mistake that for unfettered accessibility. If you are extremely accessible to your staff, then they may not be developing as they could because you are always around to solve their problems. My (Brian's) wife had to teach me this principle as our boys outgrew their lidded cups and began pouring their own juice and drinking from regular cups. I did not want to deal with the inevitable spills, so I would always encourage them to drink from the cups with lids. She reminded me that at some point they would have to learn, that it would be a mess, but that dealing with this was part of the price of parenting, of leading.

Unfortunately for us as leaders, new electronic tools and gadgets make accessibility very seductive.
General Peter Pace tells his direct reports:

Some things today—cellphones and e-mail—are not healthy for growing leaders. Before cellphones, if the boss was away, the next person in line had to make a decision. It was either right or it was wrong, but you had to accept responsibility. You learned and grew from that. Now it's too easy to call for advice. Senior leaders have to start saying, "Look, if it's not dying or burning, don't call me."[5]

Even though you are "crazy busy," as you say, do not lose hope. Stay positive, and avoid behaving like the commuters who walked by Joshua Bell because they were too busy. Keep the goal of spotting ordinary greatness first and foremost, and dream big dreams!

Notes

Chapter 1

1. Gene Weingarten, "Pearls Before Breakfast," *The Washington Post*, April 8, 2007, p. W10, www.washingtonpost.com/wp-dyn/content/article/2007/04/04/AR2007040401721.html.

2. Richard Corliss, "I Dream for a Living," *Time Magazine*, July 15, 1985, www.time.com/time/magazine/article/0,9171,959634,00.html.

3. Sir Winston Churchill, as reported on Ben Morehead's Web site, www.benmorehead.com/Churchill.html.

4. Sue Anne Pressley Montes, "In a Moment of Horror, Rousing Acts of Courage," *The Washington Post*, January 13, 2007, p. B01, www.washingtonpost.com/wp-dyn/content/article/2007/01/12/AR2007011202052.html.

5. Jay Dennis, "Ordinary Heroes Abound, Expansive Study of U.S. Rescues Shows," *Inside Illinois* 27, no. 16 (March 20, 2008), http://news.illinois.edu/ii/08/0320/index.html.

6. David Hyman, Professor of Law, University of Illinois, "Rescue without Law: An Empirical Perspective on the Duty to Rescue," *Texas Law Review* 84 (2005): 653–738, www.utexas.edu/law/journals/tlr/abstracts/84/84hyman.pdf.

7. Bob Blair, interview by Charles Gibson, "Persons of the Year," *World News with Charles Gibson,* ABC News, December 26 and June 20, 2008, http://abcnews.go.com//WN/PersonofWeek/story?id=6403273&page=1.

8. Ron Clark, interview by Oprah Winfrey, "Phenomenal Man: Mr. Clark's Opus," *O Magazine*, January 2001, www.oprah.com/article/omagazine/rys_omag_20011_phenom.

9. Walt Whitman, "A Song for Occupations," *Leaves of Grass* (Boston: James R. Osgood, 1881).

Chapter 2

1. Weingarten, "Pearls."

2. All interviews conducted in confidentiality and names withheld by mutual agreement, interviews by Pamela Bilbrey and Brian Jones, June-December 2008.

3. William Shakespeare, *Twelfth Night; or What You Will*, Act II, Scene V.

4. Dave McConnell biography, as recorded on Web site "PerfumeProjects .com," www.perfumeprojects.com/museum/marketers/Avon.php.

5. Pat MacAdam, *Gold Medal Misfits* (Manor House, 2008).

6. David Carr, "At Sundance, 'Slumdog' Casts a Long Shadow," *The New York Times*, January 16, 2009, http://movies.nytimes.com.

Chapter 3

1. Weingarten, "Pearls."

2. R. Buckminster Fuller, "Every Child Is Born a Genius," *Children's Literature Journal* 9 (1981): 3–6.

3. Tim Swanson, "Triumph of the Will," *Premiere*, December 2006, http://archive.premiere.com/features/4206/triumph-of-the-will.html.

4. Cal Fussman, "What I've Learned: Christopher Reeve," *Esquire*, December 31, 2003, www.esquire.com/features/what-ive-learned/ESQ0104-JAN_SUPERHEROES_1.

5. *Good Will Hunting*, DVD, directed by Gus Van Sant (New York: Miramax 1998).

6. Steven B. Sample, *The Contrarian's Guide to Leadership* (Jossey-Bass 2003).

7. Matthew 13:57, King James Version.

8. Blaine Smith, http://nehemiahministries.com/reshape.htm.

9. Joseph Lutz and Harry Ingham, "Johari Window," *Proceedings of the Western Training Laboratory in Group Development* (Los Angeles: UCLA, 1955).

10. Brendan Vaughan, "The Indefatigable Man," *Esquire*, March 2005, www .esquire.com/features/ESQ0305BETTER_116_2?click=main_sr.

11. Dan Lovallo, Patrick Viguerie, Robert Uhlaner, and John Horn, "Deals Without Delusions," *Harvard Business Review* 85 (12): 92–99.

12. Terrell Owens, interview by NBC sports, January 23, 2007, http://nbcsports.msnbc.com/id/16763968/.

13. Holly Brubach, "Steelers Owner Dan Rooney Turns His Business into a Family," *The New York Times*, January 27, 2009, p. B12.

14. Survey by Expedia.com, "International Vacation Deprivation Survey," 2008, http://media.expedia.com/media/content/expus/graphics/promos/vacations/expedia_international_vacation_deprivation_survey_2008.pdf.

15. Hunter S. Thompson, www.dementia.org/~strong/quotes/q_T.html.

16. William James, www.quotationspage.com/quote/23543.html.

Chapter 4

1. Weingarten, "Pearls."

2. Malcolm Gladwell, *Blink: The Power of Thinking Without Thinking* (New York: Little, Brown, and Co. 2005).

3. Bruce Morton, "Kennedy-Nixon Debate Changed Politics for Good," Web post, CNN Politics, September 26, 2005, www.cnn.com/2005/POLITICS/09/26/kennedy.nixon/index.html.

Chapter 5

1. Weingarten, "Pearls."

2. Patrick Lencioni, *The Five Dysfunctions of a Team* (San Francisco: Jossey-Bass 2002).

3. George Lebovitz and Victor Rosansky, *The Power of Alignment: How Great Companies Stay Centered and Accomplish Extraordinary Things* (John Wiley & Sons, Inc. 1997).

4. Johann Sebastian Bach, "Chaconne," *Partita No. 2 in D Minor*, 1720.

5. George Lebovitz, Op. Cit., note 3.

6. "Employees Unaware of Company Strategies," *Industry Week*, February 13, 2006, www.industryweek.com/articles/employees_unaware_of_company_strategies_11436.aspx.

7. Florence May Chadwick biography, www.answers.com/topic/florence-chadwick.

8. Jan Carlson, *Moments of Truth* (Collins Business 1989).

9. Jim Collins, *Good To Great: Why Some Companies Make the Leap and Others Don't* (New York: HarperCollins 2001).

10. David Ogilvy, *Ogilvy on Advertising* (Vintage Books USA 1985).

11. Marshall Goldsmith, "It's Not About the Coach," *Fast Company* 87 (October 2004), p. 120.

12. Anna Muoio, "The Truth Is The Truth Hurts," *Fast Company* 14 (March 1998), p. 4.

Chapter 6

1. Weingarten, "Pearls."

2. Rob Goffee and Gareth Jones, "Why Should Anyone Be Led By You?," *Harvard Business Review*, (September–October 2000).

3. Max DePree, *Leadership Is an Art* (New York: Dell 1990, reprint 2004).

4. Shawn McGrew (Service Excellence Coordinator, Freeman Health System), interview by Brian Jones, October 2008.

5. V. Clayton Sherman and Stephanie G. Sherman, *Gold Standard Management: The Key to High-Performance Hospitals* (Chicago: Health Administration Press 2008).

6. Jack and Suzie Welch, "Emotional Mismanagement," *Business Week* (July 18, 2008), www.welchway.com/Principles/Candor-(1)/Emotional-Mismanagement.aspx.

7. Brian Tracy, "Becoming a Person of Integrity," October 7, 2008, www.briantracyarticles.com/personal/becoming-a-person-of-integrity/.

8. Lao Tzu, *The Tao Te Ching*, 600 B.C., as quoted in Patrick J. and Timothy H. Warneka, *The Way of Leading People: Unlocking Your Integral Leadership Skills with the Tao Te Ching* (Asagomi Publisher International 2007).

9. "Dennis N.T. Perkins, *Leadership Lessons from the Extraordinary Saga of Shackleton's Antarctic Expedition* (New York: AMACOM, 2000).

10. T. Boone Pickens, *The Luckiest Guy in the World* (Beard Books 2000), p. 277.

11. Kate Linbaugh, "Toyota Keeps Idled Workers Busy Honing Their Skills," *The Wall Street Journal*, October 13, 2008, p. B1.

12. Stephen Covey, *The 8th Habit* (Free Press 2004).

13. Ron Crossland and Boyd Clarke, *The Leader's Voice: How Your Communication Can Inspire Action and Get Results!* (New York: Select Press 2008).

14. *An American President*, DVD, directed by Rob Reiner (California: Castle Rock Entertainment 1995).

15. Rich Karlgaard, "Peter Drucker on Leadership," *Forbes.com*, November 19, 2004.

16. Omar Kahn and Paul B. Brown, *Liberating Passion: How the World's Best Global Leaders Produce Winning Results* (John Wiley & Sons, 2008).

Chapter 7

1. Weingarten, "Pearls."

2. Edgar Powell, as quoted on the World of Quotes Web site, www .worldofquotes.com/author/Edgar-Powell/1/index.html.

3. Jack and Suzy Welch, *Winning* (New York: HarperCollins 2005).

4. Bill Taylor, interviewed by Paul Michaelman, "Why Zappos Pays New Employees to Quit—and You Should Too," *HarvardBusiness.org*, May 23, 2008, www.youtube.com/watch?v=cQLTQAv5JQA.

5. Mary Kay Ash, as quoted on Web site, www.wow4u.com/mary-kay-ash/ index.html.

6. Barbara Pagano and Elizabeth Pagano, *The Transparency Edge: How Credibility Can Make or Break You in Business* (New York: McGraw Hill 2003).

7. Keith Ferrazzi, *Never Eat Alone* (New York: Doubleday 2005).

8. Carol Patton, "Family Affair: Rewards for the Whole Family," *Incentive Magazine*, January 13, 2009.

9. Craig Ross, president of Pathways to Leadership, Inc., quoted in *Training Magazine* (July/August 2008): Margery Weinstein, "In on Onboarding," *Training Magazine*, July/August 2008, p. 8.

10. Jerome Holtzman, "How Sandberg Got Here Nearly as Classic as Career," *Chicago Tribune*, September 21, 1997, as accessed on the Daily Press Web site, http://xml.dailypress.com/news/nationworld/cs-050104 sandbergholtzman,0,2815023.story.

11. Ryne Sandberg, "Hall of Fame Induction Speech" (July 31, 2005), as recorded at the Web site Cubs.net, www.cubsnet.com/node/526.

12. Patrick Lencioni, "The Five Dysfunctions of a Team," keynote address, TEAMinar Workshop, Dallas, TX, October 8, 2003.

13. Dr. Joel Hunter (Senior Pastor, Northland Church, Florida), podcast, "Forerunners of the Kingdom," February 22, 2006.

14. Colonel Jerome Penner , 10th Mountain Division, Fort Drum, New York (Medical Services), e-mail message to author, January 27, 2009.

Chapter 8

1. Weingarten, "Pearls."

2. Patrick Hogan, "FUNdraising: Philanthropic Prodigy Rakes in Thousands, Motivates Others," *Triangle Business Journal*, February 23, 2007.

3. John Wooden, as quoted on Web site "Workinprogress.com," September 2007, http://workinprogress-workinprogress.blogspot.com/2007/09/timeless-leader.html.

4. Martin Gresty, "Graduates' experiences of the workplace (Spring 07)," as reported on prospectsnet.com, www.prospectsnet.com/cms/ShowPage/Home_page/Main_Menu___News_and_information/Graduate_Market_Trends_2007/Graduates__experiences_of_the_workplace__Spring_07_/p!ejFddpd.

5. Watson Wyatt, "Companies Worldwide Struggle to Attract, Retain Workers," watsonwyatt.com, October 22, 2007, www.watsonwyatt.com/news/press.asp?ID=18091.

6. McKinsey & Company, "Realigning the HR Function to Manage Talent," *The McKinsey Quarterly*, August 2008.

7. Father James Keller, *You Can Change the World: Anniversary Edition* (originally published 1948; Anniversary Ed., *The Christophers* 2009).

Chapter 9

1. Weingarten, "Pearls."

2. Richard Bach, *Jonathan Livingston Seagull* (Avon Books 1970), p. 34.

3. Edgar S. Cahn and Jonathon Rowe, *Time Dollars: The New Currency That Enables Americans to Turn Their Hidden Resource—Time—Into Personal Security and Community Renewal* (Rodale 1992).

4. Carl Honore, *In Praise of Slowness: How a Worldwide Movement Is Challenging the Cult of Speed*, (San Francisco, CA: HarperCollins Publications, Inc. 2004).

5. Jody Miller, "Get A Life!," *Fortune Magazine*, November 28, 2005, http://money.cnn.com/magazines/fortune/fortune_archive/2005/11/28/8361955/index.htm.

6. William Least Heat-Moon, *Blue Highways: A Journey into America* (Little, Brown, & Co. 1982).

7. Benjamin Franklin, biography, as recorded at the Franklin Institute's Web site, http://sln.fi.edu/franklin/inventor/inventor.html.

8. Peter Drucker, as quoted on Philosophers' Notes, http://philosophersnotes.com/quotes/by_topic/Forest.

9. Dana Bowman's official Web site, www.danabowman.com/danabowman12007_006.htm.

10. J. Jenkins, "Who is Reading Books?," Jenkins Group, as cited in EmpowerNet, http://empowernetinternational.com/.

11. Nicholas Carr, "Is Google Making Us Stupid?" *The Atlantic*, July/August 2008, www.theatlantic.com/doc/200807/google.

12. Irving L. Janus, *Victims of Groupthink*, (Boston: Houghton Mifflin Company 1972).

13. Linda Tischler, "A Designer Takes On His Biggest Challenge Ever," *Fast Company* 132, January 16, 2009, www.fastcompany.com/magazine/132/a-designer-takes-on-his-biggest-challenge-ever.html.

14. Jenny Uglow, *The Lunar Men: Five Friends Whose Curiosity Changed the World* (Farrar, Straus, and Giroux 2003).

15. Earl and Diana Nightingale, "Pumpkin in a Jug," from their official Web site "EarlNightingale.com," http://earlnightingale.com/store/index.cfm/fuseaction/ feature.display/feature_id/7/index.cfm?fuseaction=feature.print&feature_id=7.

16. Oral Lee Brown and Caille Millner, *The Promise* (New York: Bantam Dell Publishing Group 2005).

17. Julius Caesar, *Commentaril de Bello Civili*, (Commentaries on the Civil War), 2.8 (50s or 40s B.C.).

18. D.A. Kolb, *Experiential Learning* (Englewood Cliffs, NJ: Prentice-Hall 1984), as sourced at changingminds.org, http://changingminds.org/explanations/ learning/kolb_learning.htm.

19. Fred Epstein, M.D. and Josh Horowitz, *If I Get to Five: What Children Can Teach Us About Courage and Character* (Macmillan 2004).

20. Mike Rowe, "Seven Dirty Habits of Highly Effluent People," *Fast Company* 122, February 2008, www.fastcompany.com/magazine/122/seven-dirty-habits-of-highly-effluent-people.html.

21. Ecclesiastes 9:10, NIV.

Chapter 10

1. Weingarten, "Pearls."

2. Tim Sanders, *Love is the Killer App: How to Win Business and Influence Friends* (Random House 2002).

3. Linda Tischler, "Nissan Motor Company," *Fast Company* 60, June 2002, www .fastcompany.com/magazine/60/nissan.html.

4. Ibid.

5. David Oxberg, as quoted in "Listening with Understanding and Empathy," www.habits-of-mind.net/listening.htm.

6. Lao Tzu, *The Tao Te Ching*, 600 B.C., as quoted in Patrick J. and Timothy H. Warneka, *The Way of Leading People: Unlocking Your Integral Leadership Skills with the Tao Te Ching* (Asagomi Publisher International 2007).

7. Lawrence M. Fisher, "Richard Semler Won't Take Control," *Strategy & Business*, Winter 2005, www.strategy-business.com/press/16635507/05408.

8. Steve Jobs, *iCon: Steve Jobs, The Greatest Second Act in the History of Business*, (John Wiley & Sons 2005).

9. Kim Slack, "Leading During a Recess: When the Economy Improves, Will Your Business Be on Top?," *Forum Transforming Performance* 2008, with references to articles as follows: Pallavi Gogoi, "Circuit City Gives Up the Fight,"

BusinessWeek, May 9, 2008; and James Covert, "Earnings Outage Hits Circuit City Shares," *The New York Post*, December 22, 2007.

10. Kate Linbaugh, "Toyota Keeps Idled Workers Busy Honing Their Skills," *The Wall Street Journal*, October 13, 2008, p. B1, http://online.wsj.com/article/SB122384818385826909.html.

11. Tom Rohrs, "Fast Talk: Smarter Moves for Tougher Times," *Fast Company* 55, January 2002, www.fastcompany.com/magazine/55/fasttalk.html?page=0%2C0.

12. John Kenneth Galbraith, as quoted in "Famous Quotes on Leadership," 12Manage.com Web site, www.12manage.com/quotes_l.html.

Closing Comments

1. Lance Secretan, *One: The Art and Practice of Conscious Leadership* (Secretan Center 2006).

2. President Barack Obama, excerpt from the inaugural address, January 20, 2009: President Barack Obama, Presidential Inaugural Address, January 21, 2009, as transcribed in *The New York Times*. Available at NYTimes.com, www.nytimes.com/2009/01/20/us/politics/20text-obama.html.

Appendix B

1. Jim Collins, "Jim Collins on Tough Calls," *Fortune,* June 27, 2005, http://money.cnn.com/magazines/fortune/fortune_archive/2005/06/27/8263408/index.htm.

2. R.D. Lang, as quoted on The Quotations Page, www.quotationspage.com/quote/34029.html.

3. "And Maggie Makes Three," *The Simpsons* television series, Fox, original air date January 22, 1995, Season 6 Ep. 13.

4. McKinsey & Company, "Realigning the HR Function to Manage Talent," *The McKinsey Quarterly*, August 2008.

5. General Peter Pace, U.S. Marine Corps, vice chairman of the Joint Chiefs of Staff: Jerry Useem, "How I Make Decisions," *Fortune*, June 27, 2005, http://money.cnn.com/magazines/fortune/fortune_archive/2005/06/27/8263428/index.htm.

For More Information

We believe that everything you need to be successful as an organization currently exists in your workforce—open your eyes to the ordinary greatness that can propel you to extraordinary heights.

Web site

Please visit our Web site at www.ordinarygreatnessbook.com. Sign up for a free monthly newsletter full of ideas and proven techniques to help you and your organization discover, celebrate, and unleash the potential of ordinary greatness. We also invite you to share your own inspirational stories of ordinary greatness.

Keynotes, Retreats, Seminars, and Coaching/ Consulting Services

Keynotes to inspire; retreats to develop strategies; seminars to teach techniques and build skills; coaching and consulting to ensure successful implementation and drive results. To learn more about our services please contact us at info@ordinarygreatnessbook.com.

About the Authors

Pamela Bilbrey is a sought-after organizational consultant, author, international speaker, and facilitator of workshops and learning processes. Throughout her career, she has received national recognition for her professional achievements and thought leadership. Pam has authored three books and more than 50 articles on employee engagement, leadership and team development, and organizational change. Before starting her own consulting firm, Pam served as the founder and President of the Baptist Health Care Leadership Institute. She is also a consulting partner with The Table Group, where her focus is on coaching executive teams to extraordinary levels of excellence. Pam's passion is helping individuals and organizations discover their greatness. She and her husband, along with the kids, grandkids, cats, and dogs, live in sunny Pensacola, Florida.

Brian Jones has been described by his clients as "a breath of fresh air" and "the most effective consultant we've ever hired." He travels the country helping teams and organizations achieve real results with ordinary, yet great tools and advice. Brian has also spoken to audiences of leaders from around the world. Prior to founding his own consulting firm, Brian was Director of People Development at Baptist Health Care, Pensacola, Florida, and was Senior Consultant with the Baptist Leadership Institute. Brian is also a Consulting Partner of the Table Group, Patrick Lencioni's consulting firm. He lives in Gulf Breeze, Florida with his wife Melanie and their three sons, Seb, Gabe, and Sid. As a lifelong Chicago Cubs fan, Brian is hoping this is the year the Cubs practice "extraordinary greatness" and win the World Series.

Index